The Easy Life

Published in 2020 by Welbeck
An imprint of the Welbeck Publishing Group

20 Mortimer Street
London W1T 3JW

Text © Lynsey Crombie 2020
Design © Welbeck 2020

A CIP catalogue for this book is available from the British Library.

ISBN 978-1-78739-414-8

Printed in Dubai

10 9 8 7 6 5 4 3 2 1

LYNSEY CROMBIE

TV's QUEEN OF CLEAN

The Easy Life

Quick ways to clean and
manage your home all year round

WELBECK

Contents

The Easy Life

This book is not just about cleaning – it's also about running your home. I'm going to teach you how to plan your home and family life over the course of a year. You will create the perfect household cupboard with all your essentials, from cleaning products to light bulbs, and declutter the house from top to bottom. Most importantly, you will learn how to quickly clean and manage your home and – as a result – live the easy life.

We always seem to focus on the big annual "spring clean", but what about all the other seasons? Offering essential cleaning tips, home hacks and advice, I have created four seasonal chapters that will help break down your year into manageable sections. How you use the book is down to you – you can read it in one go and digest the content, or you can dip in and out throughout the year and implement each section as you go along.

At the end of each chapter, you'll get to fill in your own to-do list for the season. By the time you get to the list, you should be armed with plenty of ideas to fill it for your specific needs to quickly and easily keep your home life in order. I've added in plenty of fun checklists and interactive sections too, so you can get involved and enjoy the process.

My idea for this book is that you keep it somewhere in your home where you can easily access it. Pick it up every few weeks and tick off sections as you go, making sure you share it with other household members too – looking after a home is about working as a team.

Family life is busy, and with most families now having two working parents, the house is becoming less of a priority. Running a home does not have to be difficult if you approach it with my methods and tips in mind, and you can get a huge amount of satisfaction from doing so. There is nothing better than relaxing in a newly cleaned and organized room and admiring all your hard work.

Me

I was brought up in a clean and organized home. I have clear memories of my mum and my two nans always cleaning. Between them all, they taught me how to clean, although perhaps cleaning was in my genes! When I was young, my mum used to clean the primary school that I attended and one of my nans cleaned for wealthy people in west London where we lived, but was never ever looked down on. Cleaning, after all, is a good honest living. After I had my son Jake, I was keen to get back to work as soon as possible. I get easily bored and there were only so many baby singing groups I could cope with. When Jake was four months old and my twin daughters were at school, I started cleaning in a housing complex for older people and was able to take Jake with me. He used to sit in his car seat in the corner of the room and was so well behaved. I only did one customer's house per day, but this is where my cleaning journey began. The elderly people I cleaned for had so many tips and tricks up their sleeves – they had a treasure trove of cleaning knowledge. Before I knew it, I was lemon crazy, lining my cupboard tops with old newspapers and mixing up my own cleaning potions!

I want to share what I learned with you and help you become a more organized, happy person who doesn't have to worry about that big pile of laundry that is hidden in the cupboard. My approach to cleaning is little and often – I really don't want you to save up all your laundry and cleaning jobs for the weekend. After all, a clean house is a happy house and a family that cleans together stays together.

What I've been up to

I can't believe it was all the way in back in 2014 that I got my lucky break on Channel 4's *Obsessive Compulsive Cleaners* – still cleaning people's houses for a living, but this time in front of an audience of a few million!

These days you'll find me most weeks within the comfort of a sleek state-of-the-art studio at Television Centre as I share my tips and tricks with the UK on ITV's *This Morning*, which has always been a dream of mine. When I started out in TV, the little goal in my head was to do a cleaning demo on the show. Last year, my dream came true when I was approached and asked to do just that. I was in shock and overwhelmed but thrilled! I put together the features for the demo myself, with the help of a producer, pulled it out of the bag and was asked to be a regular.

I am incredibly proud to be the UK's most-watched cleaning expert on TV, and this has come with hard graft and pure determination. I often get asked how I got to where I am now, and my advice always is to be true to yourself, be professional and know your market. If you want to talk about cleaning, make sure you know your stuff and can give out safe, correct advice.

I feel so fortunate that life has led me on this journey – but I'm living proof that hard work and a lot of elbow grease really can make your wildest dreams a reality. Ultimately for me, be it running my own cleaning businesses, appearing on TV, or posting to my social media, it's all about connection and sharing my absolute passion for all things homecare.

Social media has been a welcoming home to me too. It's amazing to be able to share all I've learned over the years with my wonderful Instagram audience (apparently I'm the "original cleanstagrammer" as I've had my account since 2016 – which makes me a bit of an old hand in this brave new world of digital!) and I also really enjoy writing longer pieces for my website. I know lots of you have found me there too, which is just fantastic.

Last year, I achieved another personal goal and made my first TV advert, with Swan. We had the best time making the commercial, and every time I see it on TV, I break into a huge smile.

Things are continuing to grow for me. (I won't say too much now, but the cleaning trend is here to stay!) I now consider myself to be a brand with lots to offer and exciting plans in the pipeline.

I am truly grateful to everyone who takes the time to follow, watch and engage with me. Without all of you, this wouldn't be possible, and I will never forget the support that you have given me. I look forward to continuing to bring you ideas and tips to help you live a more organized, clean and easy life.

Six ways household management will change your life

The simplest of actions can make the way you manage your home much easier. I have learned so much from being in charge of my own home and cleaning business. Running a home is a little like running a business: you need to be organized and have a good structure in place, but you also need to delegate to others and not take on all the responsibility yourself.

Old habits can be hard to shift, so give yourself some time to get it right. If you have been used to doing things a certain way and have decided you now want to change to live a more organized life, be aware that this is going to take time. It's a bit like when you start going to the gym or go on a diet – you won't see changes straight away! Habits take some time to set in, so be patient and don't give up.

Coming back to an organized home at the end of the day will be fantastic for your work life, too. Having a clean living space gives you a clear mind and allows you to be far more productive in your working day – it's not helpful to be at work and worry about having nothing in for your evening meal. When you finish quite late and it's already dark and cold, all you want to do is go home and not think about rushing around a supermarket looking for an impulse meal that takes no time to cook and probably isn't the healthiest option. By keeping on top of your household management, you'll eliminate this unnecessary stress and gain amazing benefits – here are some examples.

★

1. A perfectly organized home

Having a system in place for organization – making sure every room in your home is clutter free and organized – will transform your life. The best system is to spend 10 minutes per week in each room tackling clutter zones.

Clutter zones are those areas where clutter builds up quickly. For example, the chair in your bedroom can quickly fill up with clothes you have tried

on or worn and not put away; your kitchen surfaces accumulate loose paperwork, post, and bits and pieces the kids bring in from school. Make a point of getting to these areas once a week and clearing them. This way it won't get out of hand – the bigger the clutter zone gets, the less likely you are going to want to deal with it.

No matter which way you choose to organize and declutter your home, make sure it is a system you can work to and keep in place.

Lots of shops these days sell amazing organization and storage solutions. Before you start following a household management plan, work out what you will need and grab some storage baskets, plastic tubs and bins. Add large self-adhesive white labels to the outside so everyone in your home knows what's inside. Pick up a few smaller containers that can fit inside cupboards, and use them in the bathroom for storing toiletries. In the kitchen, use them for storing cleaning supplies.

2. Empty laundry baskets

Having a good household-management system means getting a handle on your laundry. Laundry baskets overflowing can really bring you down – who really wants to spend all weekend doing the laundry when you could be enjoying quality time with your family?

Aim to do a laundry load a day and work on getting this habit right, as it will make a huge difference to the way your home is run. Ignoring your laundry can create a big mess in your home and in your mind. Laundry really shouldn't take more than 30 minutes a day.

Sort and load the machine	10 minutes
Hang or put in the dryer	10 minutes
Fold and organize	10 minutes

If these tasks are spread out over the day, you hardly notice you're actually doing your laundry – and that's a great thing.

3. Fuss-free ironing

One of the UK's most hated household tasks is ironing – it's time consuming, boring and hard work for most of us. Personally, I love ironing, but I also have a structure and enforce it, which does help! Commit to two ironing sessions a week, and try and keep to the same days if you can. Put on the radio, watch a film or listen to a podcast to take your mind off what you're doing. Invest in a good iron – a steam-generating iron can make all the difference and literally cut your ironing time in half. Choose the most awkward items and iron those first so they are out of the way, and then you will whizz through the rest.

Before you start, have a sturdy ironing board and hangers to hand and turn your phone to silent mode – a simple text message is enough to stop you in your tracks. As soon as you've finished, put the clothes back in the wardrobe or drawers straight away. Don't go off and do something else or get distracted, or you'll walk back into the room to see it all waiting to be put away, just when your motivation has evaporated and all you really want to do is sit down with a cup of tea.

★

4. A healthier, more affordable diet

If you really want to run the perfect home and up your skills, mastering daily meal planning is key. Flick through recipes, in books and online, that are quick and easy to make. Write down the seven evening meals you have chosen for the week. I tend to have four weeks' worth of meals and I rotate them to avoid getting bored.

When you plan your weekly shop, make sure you buy all the ingredients you need for these meals. Popping back and forth to the shops in the week is time consuming and you will end up spending more money than you need to, as you will likely be tempted to buy other things.

Create a simple meal planner using my template and follow it for the next four weeks. You'll soon see the benefits to your health and wallet.

★

5. Better relationships

It is not just one person's responsibility to keep the house clean and tidy. All the tasks need to be shared out and there is something everyone can do – not only will this save time, but you'll get on better as a family if everyone shares the load. Create a family task chart and give everyone jobs. Kids can set the table, help collect the laundry or take out the rubbish.

Everyone should look after their own bedrooms and be responsible for bringing back stray cups or plates and making their bed daily. Ensuring windows are opened by everyone as they get up will keep the house nice and aired and remove any smelly odours that can occur, especially in teenagers' bedrooms. A family meeting may be in order to get this right.

Everyone that lives in your home needs to help out.

Meal Planner

	WEEK 1	WEEK 2	WEEK 3	WEEK 4
MON				
TUE				
WED				
THU				
FRI				
SAT				
SUN				

★

6. Easy-going mornings

Before you go off and retire for the night, make sure you leave everything tidy and in order. A messy house is not what you want to wake up to!

Tidy up the kitchen so you have plenty of space to make your breakfast in the morning and plump up those sofa cushions. Make sure you have your clothes ready for the next day, whether you need a smart work outfit, something for the school run or gym gear. Help younger ones get their clothes out for the next day and get everyone's packed lunches prepped. All of this preparation will make it so much easier to get off on the right foot when you wake up.

Having good home-management skills means shedding a lot of unnecessary stress from your day-to-day life – and you'll never be embarrassed to invite a friend back to your home for a coffee or, even better, a glass of wine.

Kitting out your home

Over the years, we pick up many cleaning products and household gadgets, some of which hardly ever come out of the cupboard and end up taking up valuable storage space. Supermarkets these days offer far too much choice in cleaning and laundry products and it is tricky, if you like cleaning, not to be swayed to buy them all. We are all drawn to various smells and colours, so the supermarkets may be offering something for everyone, but that doesn't mean you have to go out and buy it all.

The things that clean for you need to be cleaned too.

Cleaning Caddy Checklist

Products to buy:

- ☐ Window cleaner
- ☐ All-purpose cleaner
- ☐ Washing-up liquid
- ☐ Laundry detergent
- ☐ Fabric conditioner
- ☐ Toilet bleach
- ☐ Beeswax polish

To make your own cleaning products, you need:

- ☐ Glass spray bottles and sticky labels
- ☐ Essential oils
- ☐ White wine vinegar
- ☐ Bicarbonate of soda
- ☐ Lemon juice
- ☐ Baby oil
- ☐ Tinfoil

Cleaning tools:

- ☐ Sponges
- ☐ Microfibre cloths in different colours (to avoid cross-contamination)
- ☐ Wire wool
- ☐ Rubber gloves
- ☐ Duster
- ☐ Squeegee
- ☐ Cotton buds – Look for the bamboo ones, as these are more sustainable and better for the environment

★
Cleaning caddy essentials

* Commit to products you have tried, tested and like. Try to stick with them and don't overload your cupboard with a multipurpose cleaner in 10 different fragrances – just buy the one you liked the most and that works best.

* For £15 a month you should be able to keep your home clean, saving you money for treats such as meals out, handbags and shoes. Don't forget to repurpose old bedding, towels and t-shirts as cleaning rags. It's so much better for the environment than using disposable wipes. Keep a strong heavy-duty plastic or fabric bag near your washing machine – save up all your dirty cleaning cloths and wash them together every time the bag is full.

* Your biggest expense in keeping your home clean is your vacuum cleaner. I often wonder how people years ago coped without one. I love my vacuum and can quite happily call it my friend. I remember the very first vacuum I bought – being brutally honest, it was absolutely rubbish! And the reason it was rubbish was because I bought the cheapest one I could. You are not going to get a good vacuum that will last and keep your home clean for just £50. Make sure you invest in your vacuum, as it is going to help you out the most. Go to a store and test them out before buying, read reviews, and make sure the vacuum suits the type of flooring you have in your home.

* A good vacuum will last you years. Don't forget to give it a little attention every so often: empty out the dust compartment, remove any threads from the roller head and clean the filter every other week to keep it in good working order.

* Use my Cleaning Caddy Checklist to make sure you have everything you need to keep your home spick and span. Take stock of this list once a month, making sure everything is stocked up and that your tools are nice and clean.

* Don't forget to add in a few strategically placed mini cleaning caddies around your home. Each should have an extra supply of handy microfibre cloths, which will save you from constantly going up and down the stairs in the middle of your cleaning.

Your essentials cupboard

Now that you have the perfect cleaning caddy, let's focus on what other essentials you need to properly equip your home.

* If you are lucky enough to have a utility/laundry room, this is probably the best place for your household essentials cupboard to be. But if not, dedicate space somewhere else in your home so everything you need is kept together and is easy to find. Under the sink is always a great central place. Use my Household Cupboard Checklist to make sure you've got everything.

* It's a good idea to use little baskets to keep your essentials together. For example, put safety pins, drawing pins and string in one group, and all your light bulbs in another. Attach a label listing the items within to the front of the so that when you open the cupboard, you can instantly locate the item you are looking for. Being organized saves you time and money, as you won't have to repeat-buy items you think have run out.

* Getting your cleaning and household items in order is the first step to running an organized home. Keep stock of these items and do a monthly check and stock up only where needed to save clutter and space.

Household Cupboard Checklist

- ☐ Bin liners
- ☐ Dustpan and brush
- ☐ Broom
- ☐ Mop and bucket
- ☐ Vacuum
- ☐ Hand-held vacuum
- ☐ Old toothbrushes – these are perfect for getting into those hard-to-reach areas and crevices, plus it's environmentally friendly to repurpose them
- ☐ Paintbrushes or old makeup brushes – these are great for dusting small areas, particularly if you have Lego in the house from younger children
- ☐ Light bulbs, including the ones for your oven
- ☐ Fuses
- ☐ Batteries
- ☐ Torch – you never know when you may have a power cut

- ☐ Extra rubber gloves
- ☐ String
- ☐ Sewing box, with essentials like needle and thread, Velcro and Wundaweb hem tape
- ☐ Plunger
- ☐ Large scissors
- ☐ Sellotape
- ☐ Glue
- ☐ Lint rollers
- ☐ Candles
- ☐ Drawing pins
- ☐ Safety pins
- ☐ Vacuum bags
- ☐ Laundry basket(s)
- ☐ Washing-up bowl or bucket
- ☐ Hand cream – your hands will need a little TLC after all the scrubbing

Where to start

Now all of your tools and products are ready to go, it's time to make a start on decluttering and cleaning your home, and achieving an easier life. But it's often hard to know where to begin. Before doing anything, you need to do a quick tidy-up – you can't clean a cluttered house, so keep mess to a minimum in order to keep everything clean and organized.

* Time is often against you when tidying up – use my Five-minute Challenge to get on its good side. You don't have to do every room in your house; just pick the four key rooms that are used the most and follow my simple guide.

* Mix it up – choose one bedroom a day along with the kitchen, bathroom and lounge. If you feel five minutes isn't long enough, up it slightly to six minutes. Remember: when you focus and work against the clock, you can achieve so much.

★

Five-minute Challenge

I really do swear by this. Since I started using this system, my life has become a whole lot easier. The best part is that my three kids don't mind this challenge, and happily get involved. When they were younger, I used to make it a game. If you do have younger children, this can really engage them as they try to beat "super mum".

I talk about this a lot across my social channels, so I won't go into too much detail, but the idea is that you set the timer on your phone, clock or cooker to a time which suits you. Now, I always choose five minutes because I have been using this method for years (so I am a bit of a pro), but other options are seven minutes or ten minutes. I do not recommend going over ten minutes – this is a quick challenge.

Five-minute Challenge

Daily laundry load
Empty washing machine
Hang up or put in the dryer
Put basket away

Bathroom
Open window
Wipe toilet seat
Put bleach/denture tablet in the pan
Quick rinse of shower and bath
Wipe sink
Shake bathroom mat
Change towels if dirty

Kitchen
Empty dishwasher
Wipe surfaces
Put away anything that is out of place
Quick vacuum
Wipe any spots on the floor
Wash and buff sink

Bedroom
Open window
Make bed
Pick up dirty clothes
Quick surface tidy

Lounge
Fluff up sofa cushions
Quick vacuum
Tidy up books or toys
Wipe coffee table
Fold any blankets/throws

★

How the Five-minute Challenge works

* Choose three or four rooms before you leave the house for your day at work or on the school run, etc. Four rooms are then just 20 minutes of cleaning a day. Add another 10 minutes for your daily laundry load, and at just 30 minutes total, you are returning from work or errands to a neat house.

* Use the chart on page 23 for each room, and you are going to be shocked at the amount you have done in such a small space of time.

* When you set your mind to this and are motivated, you see immediate results. Realistically, in those five minutes you could probably send a few texts or an email, but by challenging yourself to clean against the clock, you have gotten your home's basic maintenance cleaning done for the day.

Set the timer to your chosen challenge time and go, go, go!

* The added bonus of this task is that you have also had a small workout. Speed cleaning is working your whole body and burning off calories.

★

Multitask

* As well as the Five-minute Challenge, multitasking can help you quickly get on top of tidying. When you are chatting on the phone, you have a spare hand. Use it to do a bit of light dusting or tidy up some paperwork.

* While the kettle is boiling, use those three minutes to do something constructive; don't just stand there and scroll through your phone. I tend to empty the dishwasher and this seems to work out perfectly. You could also give your tiles or splashback a clean or take the rubbish out. Simple tasks like these don't take much time but will, in turn, give you time back.

* If you take baths, give the loo a quick wipe, empty the bathroom bin or have a quick tidy of your bathroom products while the bath is running.

Now you've got everything neat and tidy, use the following tools and tasks to make your perfect home management plan.

★

When's good for you?

Decide when you are most productive in the day and stick to this time slot for your chores. Are you a morning person or an afternoon person? I find my energy levels are at their highest in the mornings, so I do most of my cleaning and household chores then. Doing your cleaning early gets it out of the way, and you don't have to worry about it for the rest of the day. An elderly lady once said to me, "An hour in the morning is worth two hours in the afternoon", and that comment really stuck.

★

Create a to-do list

Sometimes I get up in the mornings and feel completely overwhelmed with all the tasks I have to fit into my day and it can cause me to become rather anxious. But over the years, I have learned that as soon as I write down all the tasks that are floating around in my head, I suddenly feel so much better.

When you create your to-do list, put priority items at the top to help ensure you complete them. Your to-do list:

* Structures your day

* Gives you less to remember

* Gives you a sense of satisfaction

* Reduces anxiety

* Encourages better time management

The satisfaction I get when I start to tick off those tasks is immense.

When creating your to-do list, go easy on yourself. It is all right not to finish everything on the list – you do always have tomorrow. Daily to-do lists are now a habitual part of my life and have definitely made household tasks more manageable.

Set a routine

There's no point in creating a plan if it is unmanageable and you can't actually achieve the tasks you have set. Make your new routine realistic for you, and include the other people who live in your home. Housework is never just down to one person, it's a team effort; the days of the 1950s housewife have well and truly disappeared. Delegation is key. Encourage everyone to look after their space and tidy up their own things.

I often think about Mrs Beeton, the original cleaning guru, and how she would have coped without any of the gadgets we have today. She wouldn't have even had a vacuum. When I was young, I remember seeing my nan using a mangle in the garden, as she didn't have a washing machine. It must have been incredibly time-consuming and difficult washing clothes and sheets in the sink and then pushing them through a mangle. We are quite spoilt these days; housework with these helpful tools, in small manageable chunks, is easy. There are loads of time-saving tools and tricks you can use to make your daily routine a walk in the park:

* We have lots of amazing household gadgets available to use these days. Make use of them if they help you speed up your cleaning. If a mop and bucket is too fiddly, use a steamer, and if hand-washing the windows is taking too long, use a window vac.

* Get into the habit of tidying up the kitchen every day after dinner. Aim to never wake up to a kitchen full of dirty dishes and uncleaned place mats still left on the dining table. After your evening meal, wipe down the kitchen surfaces and hob, load the dishwasher or do the washing-up, tidy up the table and have a quick sweep or vacuum.

* As I mentioned before, getting those annoying jobs done the night before will give you easy-going mornings. Anything you will need tomorrow morning, get ready tonight.

Daily Routine Template

Morning
- ☐ ....
- ☐ ....
- ☐ ....
- ☐ ....

Morning
- ☐ ....
- ☐ ....
- ☐ ....
- ☐ ....

Evening
- ☐ ....
- ☐ ....
- ☐ ....
- ☐ ....

Evening
- ☐ ....
- ☐ ....
- ☐ ....
- ☐ ....

Morning
- ☐ ....
- ☐ ....
- ☐ ....
- ☐ ....

Morning
- ☐ ....
- ☐ ....
- ☐ ....
- ☐ ....

Evening
- ☐ ....
- ☐ ....
- ☐ ....
- ☐ ....

Evening
- ☐ ....
- ☐ ....
- ☐ ....
- ☐ ....

Morning
- ☐ ....
- ☐ ....
- ☐ ....
- ☐ ....

Morning
- ☐ ....
- ☐ ....
- ☐ ....
- ☐ ....

Evening
- ☐ ....
- ☐ ....
- ☐ ....
- ☐ ....

Evening
- ☐ ....
- ☐ ....
- ☐ ....
- ☐ ....

Spring

Spring has finally come! Now is the time to hang up those woolly jumpers, bring out your summer shoes and trade in your hot chocolate for herbal tea.

We tend to hibernate quite a bit through the winter months, cozying up with blankets and watching endless films on the sofa by candlelight.

Spring brings a new and exciting energy to you and your living space. It's time to shake off those winter blues, but it's not always obvious where to start. After enduring the winter weather, the outside of the home is always a good place to begin repairing and refreshing.

The best thing about spring is the return of blue skies and fluffy white clouds, boosting your mood and providing you with the ideal working background. Put on an upbeat and motivational playlist and go for it!

Spring cleaning is good for you!

Whether you love it or hate it, there's no denying that a good spring clean can be a worthwhile exercise. It can also boost your health and wellbeing. Here are five of my favourite benefits:

★

1. Fewer lost items

Making the effort to declutter and organize your home or office in the big spring clean can save you time looking for or replacing lost items in the future. The stress caused when a family member has lost something important can be overwhelming, and can then spur family arguments. When decluttering with your spring clean, ensure you let go of items you don't need or haven't used. Create useful, organized spaces for the items you need and decide to keep.

★

2. Keeps allergens at bay

It'll probably come as no surprise to you that deep cleaning helps to remove allergens from your home. Doing a deep clean just as spring begins can help alleviate the constant sneezing and sniffling that signals the start of hay fever season.

★

3. Boosts happiness

The act of cleaning your home to a great standard helps foster a feeling of pure satisfaction and, I find, puts you in a great mood. When cleaning, I always listen to upbeat, positive music and recommend moving your body as much as you can! There is no harm in having a little boogie with your feather duster or a spin around your kitchen with your mop, and the endorphins your brain releases as you exercise will improve your mood even further.

A tidy house equals a tidy mind.

★

4. Reduces stress levels

Cleaning and organizing your personal spaces lets you enjoy a tidier and more organized environment at home, and this can relieve stress.

Levels of stress can also be reduced during the act itself, as cleaning is considered to be therapeutic. Whenever I feel low, I always go into cleaning overdrive and it's remarkable how much better I feel afterwards.

★

5. Focus

When you clear out the clutter, you free up your brain. This renewing effect allows you to make better, more productive decisions so that you can excel in your workplace and at home.

First steps

Spring cleaning came about years ago when people didn't have the vast choice of cleaning tools that we have today. The Victorians used to hire someone to come to their house to do the vacuuming with a huge contraption called the "domestic cyclone", which ran on petrol. It was ferried around from home to home on a horse and cart, sucking up dust and debris with a long hose that was snaked in through the windows!

When you're in spring-cleaning mode you want to throw open those windows and really go for it. Although spring cleaning traditionally starts on 5 March, it's often too cold for us to start this annual rite – so, the school holidays in April are a good time to get cleaning, especially if you take time off of work for them already. Plus, you'll have a few extra pairs of little hands to help!

Spring cleaning is really just one big deep clean – if you keep on top of your housework, you are already halfway there, but every home benefits from a thorough deep clean and it's about getting to those places that you are missing in your regular clean. Once you have finished, your home will smell and look sparkling, and you'll know exactly where everything is.

Plan

It can be tough finding the motivation for what seems like a huge task. The key is planning.

* Plan a day or two in your diary for your spring clean and stick to it: keep the entire day free. Avoid getting in your own way – don't arrange to meet a friend for lunch, because when you come back, you won't feel motivated.

* Walk around your home and make a list of all the tasks that need to be done. Ticking these off as you get through them is always a great feeling.

* List any redecorating tasks, as some of your rooms may have taken quite a lot of wear and tear over the winter months.

Distractions

Remove any distractions that may interrupt your plan. Your phone is probably the biggest distraction; as soon as you get a text or social-media alert, you will lose time, as that text often turns into a conversation and the social-media alert prompts you to look through everyone's daily status.

* First things first: switch your phone to aeroplane mode.

* Keep the TV off! Daytime TV may just grab your attention enough that you sit down with a cup of tea and a biscuit.

* Knock, knock. If you are expecting a delivery, answer the door. But if you aren't, don't answer. It may be a friend stopping by for a coffee and catch-up on the off chance you are in, and you certainly don't have time for this.

Visualize how great your home will look once you have finished.

* Keep your mind positive and think of the end result, not the pile of clutter in the corner.

Music

You need some motivation to keep you going, so download fun, uplifting and motivating playlists that will last the duration of your clean. Choose songs that make you want to move your body. Remember: cleaning is also great exercise, and your big spring clean will certainly burn some calories and even tone up those arms.

Support

Make sure you involve the whole family – including the children – in the big spring clean this year.

* Spring cleaning, like daily home cleaning, is not just down to one person. It's a family affair, so divide the home up into sections and all agree on a section each. Remember to include the garage, shed and garden on your spring-clean checklist.

* If you are making use of those little hands by involving the children, then make it a game for the younger ones. Crank up those tunes and get them dancing around with you while you do the dusting.

* Play to your family's strengths so you are getting the best from them. One may love to organize desk drawers and books, and another may enjoy running the vacuum around. If they enjoy it, they are more likely to stick to it and help you out.

* Give them their own list with specific tasks that are safe and easy for them to do. You can also make it a bit of a competition between them so they work faster and harder.

* Incentivize their work with a reward – a family day out or other special event. After a few hard days helping you, they deserve to look forward to a treat.

★

Be ready

Have all your tools and products ready. The vacuum should be empty and raring to go, and all your cloths washed. Make sure your cleaning caddy is stocked with your favourite products, and that you have on comfortable clothes, rubber gloves and your apron.

One last thing: do not forget to have a good breakfast. Cleaning burns a lot of calories and is best fuelled by a big bowl of porridge or some eggs on toast to start the day. Keep some snacks like granola bars and fresh fruit handy to replenish your energy as the day goes on.

Use my Spring-cleaning Checklist to help you, or make your own list. If you really can't face it all in one go, fill in the 30-day Spring-cleaning Challenge using the template on page 39 and do one item a day for a month.

Spring-cleaning Checklist

- ☐ Tackle all those cobwebs
- ☐ Clean the front door and garage, and sweep any leaves
- ☐ Take down curtains and wash, or take to the dry cleaners
- ☐ Clean your vacuum cleaner
- ☐ Have a sort through under-bed storage and vacuum
- ☐ Wash/polish all internal doors
- ☐ Clean out the first aid cupboard, stock check and replenish
- ☐ Switch winter-scented candles and diffusers to spring ones
- ☐ Sort through winter shoes and boots, store them and swap for summer shoes
- ☐ Switch clothes from winter to spring, using vacuum-sealed bags for storage
- ☐ Clean appliances thoroughly, including sides and plugs
- ☐ Deep clean your fridge and cupboards
- ☐ Wash bed throws and bath mats
- ☐ Wash hats, gloves and scarves – store away until next winter
- ☐ Wash or dry clean winter coats and store them away

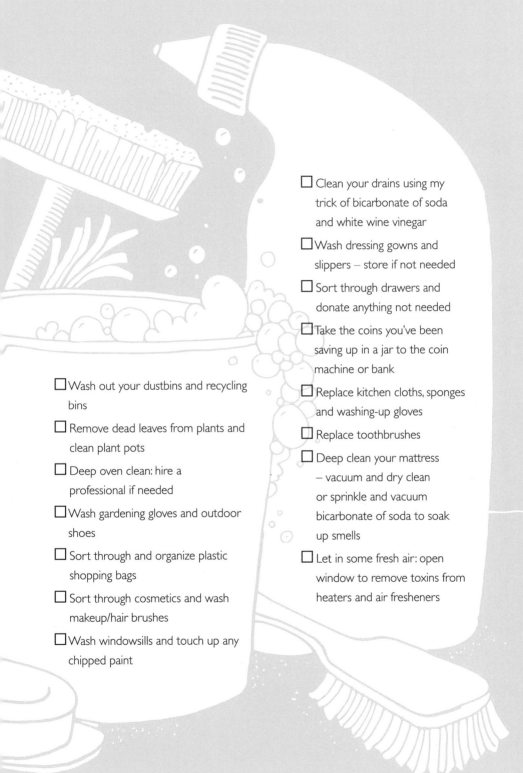

- [ ] Clean your drains using my trick of bicarbonate of soda and white wine vinegar
- [ ] Wash dressing gowns and slippers – store if not needed
- [ ] Sort through drawers and donate anything not needed
- [ ] Take the coins you've been saving up in a jar to the coin machine or bank
- [ ] Replace kitchen cloths, sponges and washing-up gloves
- [ ] Replace toothbrushes
- [ ] Deep clean your mattress – vacuum and dry clean or sprinkle and vacuum bicarbonate of soda to soak up smells
- [ ] Let in some fresh air: open window to remove toxins from heaters and air fresheners

- [ ] Wash out your dustbins and recycling bins
- [ ] Remove dead leaves from plants and clean plant pots
- [ ] Deep oven clean: hire a professional if needed
- [ ] Wash gardening gloves and outdoor shoes
- [ ] Sort through and organize plastic shopping bags
- [ ] Sort through cosmetics and wash makeup/hair brushes
- [ ] Wash windowsills and touch up any chipped paint

30-day Spring-cleaning Challenge

1	2	3
7	8	9
13	14	15
19	20	21
25	26	27

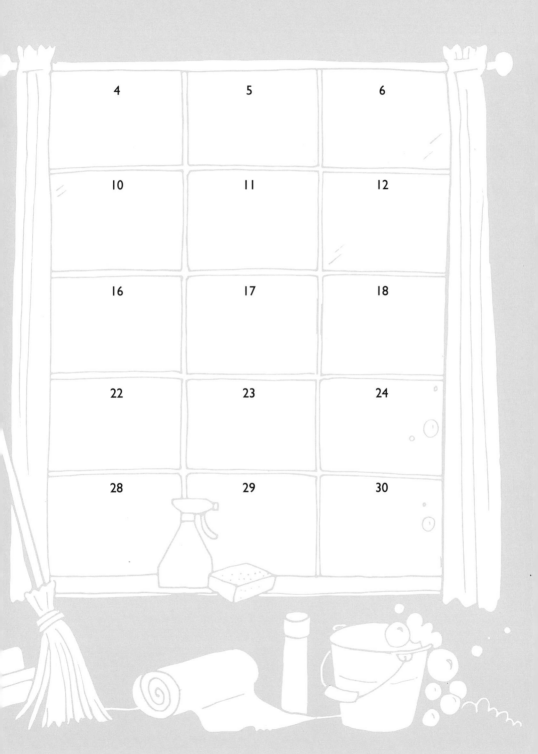

Beds

* Flip and rotate your mattresses, vacuum them with a crevice tool and deodorize them. Treat any stains with a spot-stain treatment and leave to air for the whole day if you can.

* Switch your duvet from winter to summer, if applicable, and pack away the heavier duvet in a vacuum-sealed bag. Air your new duvet by hanging it over the washing line in the fresh air and sunshine for a few hours. It's been in storage for possibly six months, so it needs bringing back to life! You can also use a dry-cleaning duvet solution at home in your tumble dryer, which works well if your drum is big enough to fit your duvet.

* Although pillows and cushions are covered with cases and protectors, they do still need to be cleaned at least two to three times a year. Most can be chucked into the washing machine and laid flat to air-dry, but check the manufacturer's instructions.

* Nothing looks worse on a bed than a flat, misshapen pillow. Those yellow stains we sometimes get are caused by sweat. When your face or head rests against the pillow for a long period of time, it sweats through the pillowcase into the pillow. Moisture from wet hair also can cause these yellow stains, as well as the chemicals from skin-care, fake-tan products and make-up.

Rugs

You may run your vacuum over your rug a few times a week, but this isn't always enough, especially if you have a deep-pile rug. Back in Victorian times, rugs were beaten to release all the dirt and then hung outside in the freezing-cold air to keep them fresh and looking new. These days we just run the vacuum over them most of the time.

* Before you use a carpet cleaner to spring-clean your rug, flip it over and vacuum all over the back of the rug. This pushes out ground-in dirt, dust and debris.

★

Sofa

You may vacuum your sofa weekly, but when it comes to the big spring clean more attention is needed. From eating TV dinners to watching a film with your pet snuggled up against you, the sofa is an integral part of the home. It can capture body oils, cooking odours, dust mites and pet dander, causing allergies and irritation to airways. Eating on your sofa isn't ideal because food particles, marks from sticky fingers and spilt drinks can all easily occur when you're enjoying a snack.

* Remove your sofa covers if you can and either stick in the washing machine or take to the dry cleaner as appropriate – always check the label for instructions. For any tough stains that are still present, mix together ¾ cup warm water, ¼ cup white wine vinegar and one tablespoon of washing-up liquid. Scrub the mixture in with a hard brush and then blot dry.

A few simple changes can really lift a room.

* If you have cushion covers that can come off, pop them in the washing machine and follow the guidelines on the cushion's tag.

* A light steam with a clothes steamer over your sofa will kill germs and help to keep allergies at bay.

★

Refresh

During your spring clean, it's a good time to give some of your rooms that are looking tired and out of date a little refresh. You don't have to spend much money to get a new look.

* Brighten up with new lighting; if you've had your eye on an antique lamp or fun lampshade, why resist the urge any longer? A new lamp can make it feel like a brand-new room. You can install strip lighting above cabinets, or redirect your existing lighting to highlight particular features of the room.

* Don't forget to swap out any cushions and throws so they match your seasonal bedding, or simply replace cushion covers. You can refresh the whole colour scheme of a room with just a few soft furnishings – an inexpensive upgrade.

* Give your windows something new to wear. Ready-to-hang window curtains are easy to install and create an instant lift to the room, or consider changing the curtain pole to create a fresher look.

* Lastly, open up a room. It's an old trick, but it works every time: hang up a large mirror, and watch a small room transform to give the illusion of a bigger room.

★

Look after your tools

When spring cleaning, don't forget to look after the things that clean for you:

* Handheld and upright vacuums.

* Window vac – This sucks dirt from the outside windows, so it needs a rinse.

* Washing machine – Clean inside the drum and run a hot cycle with white wine vinegar.

* Dishwasher – Rinse the filter and give the whole thing a good once-over before running a rinse cycle with lemon juice.

* Tumble dryer – Regularly clean the filter and drum of your tumble dryer. See page 158–9 for instructions.

Infrequent Tasks Checklist

Remember, spring cleaning is also about including those rare tasks we don't include in our weekly cleaning schedules.

- ☐ Carpet cleaning – invest in your own and use a few times a year; you could even split the cost and share with a local family member or friend. Alternatively, hire an outside company or a machine from a supermarket to deep clean your carpets.

- ☐ Extractor fans – these collect a lot of dust, the build-up of which can prevent them working well. Use a small brush – an old mascara wand or toothbrush – and remove that dust.

- ☐ Plant care – refresh plants by adding a little new soil to the top. If the plant looks like it has outgrown its pot, re-pot it in a slightly larger container.

- ☐ Dust your walls and ceiling – use a long-handled flathead duster, the kind you'd usually clean the floor with, and reach up high to remove dust from walls and the ceiling. Remember that dust falls, so you will need to vacuum afterwards.

- ☐ Move furniture – pull out the sofa and any other furniture that you can handle and clean behind them. It will be rather dusty under there if the area hasn't been touched for a while. If you have any electrical switches behind your furniture, I bet they have a layer of dust too. Turn them off at the socket and clean.

- ☐ Dust books – these pick up a layer of dust if they haven't been touched in a while.

- ☐ Window and door tracks – These often-overlooked spaces can be sorted out with a small brush or toothbrush to remove the debris and mud. Follow up with a hand vac to collect the dirt.

- ☐ Cupboards – Take everything out of your kitchen and bathroom cupboards and sort through the items you have. Disinfect the empty cupboards with a diluted vinegar solution. They may be a little sticky or have food crumbs – use your hand vac to get these up and wipe over any sticky patches.

Outside your home

First impressions count, and the lead-up to your front door is important because it says a lot about you and your family. A front door needs to be welcoming and should reflect who you are.

* Make sure the door and windows are gleaming – the entrance should already receive a once-over weekly. For a spring clean, pay attention to your letterbox and any other brass fittings, such as the door knocker and the hinges.

* You certainly don't need to have green fingers to keep your home looking bright and colourful. Buy a few nice but inexpensive hanging baskets or flower pots and fill them with low-maintenance flowers such as pansies, sweet peas and Busy Lizzies for a spot of colour.

* A doormat with a simple welcome message can also be a nice addition to your front entrance, greeting guests and reminding them to wipe their shoes at the same time!

* If your doorbell has stopped working over the winter months, now is the time to get this fixed or replaced.

★

Keep weeds at bay

* Keep the front path and walkway up to your home weed free. There's something therapeutic about ripping up a troublesome weed before it has the chance to terrorize your lawn and garden.

Forget nasty chemicals and just pour boiling water onto weeds.

* Prune those overgrown garden shrubs. Snipping away the dead bits makes way for new healthy growth.

* After you've seen to the entrance, now is the time to inspect the rest of the outside of your home.

Fencing and boundaries

* Remove any cobwebs with a brush and apply a quick lick of paint if necessary. If you have metal railings, you can wash these down with warm soapy water. Check any type of fence post by giving it a quick wiggle to make sure it is still secure and safe.

* Rot is the biggest thing to look for in a wooden fence. If it's been a few years since the wood has been treated, check to see if bugs have gnawed their way into any part of it. If so, you may have to replace some or all of the fence.

De-leaf your lawn

Your outside space has spent the winter feeling cold and abandoned. Get ready for a lush lawn and a flourishing garden by getting rid of the soggy, old leaves choking your flowerbeds and grass.

★

Outside drains

Even if these are not blocked or smelling, they still need a little attention. Flush those drains you can access with boiling water and soda crystals.

★

Security lights

Check that these are in working order and wipe over their exterior with warm soapy water.

★

Gutters

Use a secure ladder and get rid of any leaves, twigs and gunk to ensure your gutters are running freely and have no overgrown moss or other obstructions. Wear gardening gloves to avoid hurting yourself! If any have been damaged from the cold weather and winds, get these fixed. Broken gutters can look very untidy and bring the appearance of your home down.

★

Paths and paving

If you are lucky enough to own a pressure or power washer, give your paving a good blast. Alternatively, use a good hard broom along with warm soapy water. For any stubborn stains, use a concrete-cleaning solution that you can get from most DIY stores.

★

Dustbins

Keep these clean throughout the year, but give them a much deeper clean now, focusing on the wheels and the whole of the outside. Spray your bins with disinfectant and leave to sit for a while. Rinse with hot water, or use a power washer. Pay attention to the lid and the area the bin sits in, and check for any fallen rubbish. Smear the lid after cleaning with an environmentally friendly oil such as citronella, tea tree or eucalyptus to keep bugs away.

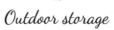

Outdoor storage

Outhouses tend to be huge, cluttered cupboards with bits and bobs that have no real home strewn everywhere. Most people tend to chuck all their unwanted stuff into these spaces – so at least it is out of the house – with the intention of one day taking it to the skip or charity shop, or listing it on a selling site. Spring is the ideal time to start to organize and clear your garage space. Once the summer hits, you don't want to be wasting your time hunting for the paddling pool or sprinkler.

Outhouses make good storage for toxic materials such as weed killers and paints, but chemicals need to be properly labelled and stored and locked away from children and pets.

Make sure you have good security on your outhouse or garage, as most of the equipment and belongings you have in these areas is expensive. So many people forget to lock garages and sheds, making them a real treat for any burglars out there.

Use my Garage and Shed Checklist to declutter and clean out these spaces.

* Before you get started, you need to plan. Outhouse organizing and decluttering is a big job. It may be worth working as a family and setting aside a day, or asking a few friends or neighbours to help.

* Choose a day with good weather so that you can get as many things outside onto your drive as possible.

* Look at what you actually have in these areas and decide on the zones you want to implement in the garage space. These could include:

  * Hobby area   * Laundry area (if applicable)

  * Gardening tools   * Decorating and work tools

  * Bikes and kids' toys

Garage and Shed Checklist

- ☐ Remove everything from the garage or shed and onto the drive or lawn, organizing it by zone – this will make putting everything back much easier.

- ☐ Arrange your outdoor furniture – this will stay outside until autumn.

- ☐ Clean any stains or dirt from the floor. Motor-oil stains are probably the biggest stains in the garage and can look unsightly. To remove, cover with cat litter or sawdust and leave for a few minutes. Prepare a bowl of warm water, add plenty of washing-up liquid and use a wire brush to scrub the stain away. Sweep up the excess cat litter or sawdust.

- ☐ Knock off any cobwebs that tend to be all over garages with a large broom and then sweep them away.

- ☐ If you have any mould patches around the window, tackle them with a vinegar and water mixture.

- ☐ Clean the walls with a warm soapy water solution and a large sponge. To reach higher spots, use a flat-headed mop.

- ☐ Sweep the floor to get rid of the dust you've shaken loose. Mop and hose the floor. Leave the floors for two to four hours to dry.

- ☐ Organize some storage – install cabinets, shelves, racks and hooks.

- ☐ Use labelled boxes, baskets and old plastic storage containers from the kitchen to organize – adhesives in one box, wrapping paper in another, paint cans on the shelves, etc.

- ☐ Use wall hooks to hold larger tools such as rakes and shovels, or stand these items up in a large, sturdy bin.

- ☐ Use a pegboard to organize hand tools such as hammers and hacksaws.

- ☐ Just like your front door, the garage door needs to be clean and tidy too. Start off by brushing the door down using a long-handled broom, removing all the cobwebs and debris from over the winter months. Rinse the door with your garden hose or power washer.

- ☐ Take a good-sized sponge and bucket of warm soapy water and wipe the garage door down. Buff dry with an old rag to prevent any smears.

My guide to cleaning those awkward appliances in your home

The final stage in your spring clean is to make sure you've done all of those niggly, unpleasant jobs that you've been putting off for months. One of the most unpopular jobs is cleaning appliances – but it's so important to get into all those nooks and crannies and look after those everyday tools that look after you.

Toaster

* Always unplug your toaster before cleaning it. Take out the crumb tray, empty it into the bin or food compost and wash it in warm soapy water in the sink. Turn the toaster upside down and bash the crumbs out over the bin or onto a sheet of newspaper.

* Clean off any burn marks with a paste of bicarbonate of soda and water. Apply using a microfibre cloth, rub in and leave for five minutes, and then wipe off and buff dry for a super shine.

Microwave

My favourite way of cleaning the microwave is to place four slices of lemon into a microwave-safe bowl of water and then cook on high for three minutes. The steam from the water and lemon loosens stuck-on foods and grease and kills any nasty odours. Then wipe clean with a damp microfibre cloth.

Cooker hood filters

These can get really sticky, and they hold onto odours that can, in turn, make your kitchen smell. Make a point to take this filter out regularly and soak in a sink of hot water with a few capfuls of white wine vinegar to break down the grease build-up and odours.

★

Taps

* It's incredibly easy for limescale to build up on your taps. My top tip for this is to cut a lemon in half, cover it with bicarb and give it a squeeze so that it foams up. Rub all over the tap and finish by twisting the lemon half onto the spout. Leave for 15 minutes and then remove the lemon and rinse off the juice – the limescale will come off easily. Buff dry.

* In the regular cleaning of your taps, wipe with warm soapy water and buff dry with a clean microfibre cloth. Most taps are made from chrome, but if your taps have an unusual finish, follow the manufacturer's instructions.

★

Hob toppers

If you don't know what these are, these are the little black toppers on your hob which get covered in burned-on food from spillages and splashes. Place them in a reusable plastic sandwich bag, sprinkle them with bicarbonate of soda, add a splash of white wine vinegar and vigorously shake the bag. Pop it on the side and leave for 15 minutes, and watch as the liquid changes to brown and all the mess is lifted away.

★

Bread bin

This is one of those items that we can forget to clean, but breadcrumbs can build up in them quickly. They hold food we will consume, so it's a good idea to give it a weekly rinse with warm soapy water.

★

Smoothie maker

Once used, give the smoothie cup a quick rinse under the tap. Then add a small squirt of washing-up liquid, half fill with water and put the cup back onto the base of the blender and turn on for 10 seconds. This gives the cup a thorough clean and ensures the blades are clean too. It's a quick and easy way to clean that avoids any potential accidents with the blades.

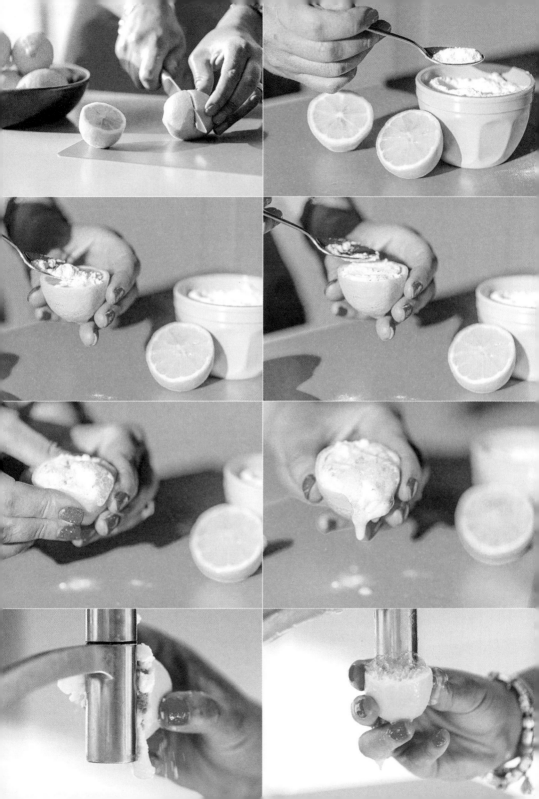

★

Washing machine

* When your machine is not in use, try to leave the detergent tray open slightly just so this gets some air and dries out. This little tray gets wet regularly and never really gets the chance to dry out. Once a week take your tray out and soak it in warm soapy water and then dry it well before you pop it back in. Also clean the space it comes from, putting your arm right in and giving it a good clean and dry.

* Run a quick cycle or white wine vinegar weekly. This helps keep any mould build-up at bay and neutralizes any nasty odours. I then use a shop-bought washing machine cleaning solution monthly.

* Give the rubber seal a good wipe. You can use your detergent for this or mix some bicarbonate of soda with some white wine vinegar into a paste and use a small brush to get right into the rubber. The rubber seal picks up all sorts of dirt from your clothes and will also pick up minerals and hard water.

* The filter at the bottom of your machine will need to be emptied regularly too – try to do this at least once a month. Plus, if you can access the back of your machine easily, check the water supply pipe for any build-up of dirt.

★

Dishwasher

* Empty the filter of your dishwasher (mine simply twists and pulls). You can find how to do this in your instruction manual or on your washer manufacturer's website.

* Wipe down all your seals and around the door with a solution of 50% white wine vinegar, 20% neat lemon juice and 30% water. I put the solution in a spray bottle, so it can be used for other household cleaning jobs. Lemon juice leaves a fresh, clean smell and lemons are also great for breaking down dirt and grime.

* Place a cup of white wine vinegar mixed with lemon juice in the top of your dishwasher and run it on a hot cycle – this helps get rid of any grease and gunk.

* Once the cycle has completed, sprinkle the bottom of your dishwasher with bicarbonate of soda, which is excellent at eliminating any nasty smells.

★

Dishwasher loading tips

* Always try to load your dishwasher correctly for maximum efficiency.

* The top shelf is for your cups and glasses. A top tip here is to place glasses next to cups and alternate, in order to stop the glasses from scratching each other. Make sure glasses and cups are turned upside down so that the water drains – if they are upright, dirty water will sit in them.

* The bottom section is for your plates, bowls and pans. Place all your cutlery in the basket, facing downwards to avoid any potential accidents.

★

Kitchen bin

Wipe the lid and sides weekly. When you change the bag, sprinkle bicarbonate of soda into the bottom to help soak up any nasty odours. Alternatively, slice up some lemon and pop this in the bottom too.

Once a month, you should give your dishwasher a clean.

Spring To-do List

Priority tasks

....
....
....
....
....
....
....
....
....
....
....

Texts and emails to send

....
....
....
....
....
....
....
....
....

Shopping list (food and household essentials)

....
....
....
....
....
....
....
....
....
....
....

Phone calls to make

....
....
....
....
....
....
....

Cleaning tasks

....
....
....
....
....
....
....
....
....

What's for tea?

....
....
....
....
....
....
....
....
....
....

NOTES

....
....
....
....
....
....
....
....
....
....

Summer

Summer is my absolute favourite season. I love the fact that my home seems to appear bigger as the garden becomes an extra room.

When the first signs of summer start to appear, it's time to start thinking about outdoor fun. We all love barbecues, days spent at the park with a delicious picnic and weekend trips to the seaside. Summer is only for a short time, so we need to enjoy it and not waste time inside cleaning and organizing. We have just had the big spring clean, so your home should be pretty spick and span.

Equally, summer does bring with it some cleaning-related mishaps, from ketchup all over your new white top to carpet stains thanks to the constant back and forth to the garden.

It also brings holiday packing and organizing, which can sometimes be tricky, especially if you're working long hours and panicking about how to fit it in. The family summer holidays are a little easier when you have a few of my tricks up your sleeve!

Summer hacks and cleaning tips

★

Easy sand removal

Baby powder makes it really easy to get sand off your skin. Carry a small bottle of baby powder with you to the beach this summer – it'll help everyone get sand free before they climb back into the car by simply sprinkling the baby powder over bottoms of legs and feet and rubbing the mixture off.

★

Hamburger helper

When you're eating burgers off the BBQ this summer, try eating them upside down instead. The top of a hamburger bun is usually a bit thicker than the bottom, so it holds up better with all those toppings and sauces. No more struggling with crumbling burger buns and embarrassing sauce drips.

★

Swimwear

Swimwear can often quickly discolour over the summer months and lose its shape from all the wringing out. To keep your family's swimwear from becoming faded or warped, rinse it out as soon as you can – strong chemicals from swimming pools and saltwater from the sea contribute to fading. Once rinsed, rather than wringing it out, place the swimwear into a folded towel and stamp on it or press down to expel excess water. Then, hang it to dry – but not in direct sunlight.

★

Fake-tan stains

Fake-tan products are becoming more popular and are whipped out the instant the sun makes an appearance. A quick fix to remove fake tan is to make a paste out of bicarbonate of soda and lemon juice and apply directly to the stain. Scrub in a circular motion until the stain starts to disappear.

Beach towels

We put our beach towels through a lot over summer, and they can start to smell a little funky. When you're on holiday, a washing machine isn't always available. If your beach towels could use some freshening up, never fear! There's a simple process that gets them smelling great. Make up my homemade fabric refresher (see page 188) and take it on holiday with you. Between airing the towels outside and spritzing them, they will stay smelling fresh.

Plastic toys

Toys that get left outside can become dirty and mouldy quite quickly. Pop them in a bowl of warm soapy water and add in a drop of white wine vinegar.

Dust more often

Letting the sun shine through your windows fills your home with beautiful, natural light. Unfortunately, it can also fill your home with dust! Being around dust can trigger an allergic reaction, which can prevent you from enjoying the summer. To avoid this problem, make an effort to dust more regularly during the summer. A damp microfibre cloth every few days can work just as well as a shop-bought polish – or use a handheld vacuum to speed the dusting process up so you can get outside and enjoy the sunshine.

Prevent mildew and mould growth

Mould and mildew grow faster in humid summer weather, especially in areas of your home that are already humid, such as the bathroom. Spray some neat white wine vinegar on any mould patches, leave for 30 minutes and then rinse. Without the need for any scrubbing, the mould will vanish.

Ice cream hacks

* Paper or foil cupcake liners help catch drips for messy little ones. Pop a hole into the liner and slide the stick in until it reaches the base of the lolly or ice cream. This will hold onto any drips and save them from dripping onto clothes. Alternatively, place a large marshmallow on the stick, which both catches the drips and is delicious to eat!

* I hate it when my kids ask for ice cream, because I just don't have the arm power to get it out! But you can avoid this by placing your ice-cream tub into a freezer-safe bag before freezing – this will keep it soft.

Flip your mattress

Most mattresses today have a winter side and a summer side; the material covering each side is different, designed for different conditions. Whether or not your mattress has designated sides, keep in mind that summer is the best time to clean a mattress – the temperature is high and everything dries quickly, eliminating the risk of mould or mildew growth on the fabric.

Stop that smelly washing machine

* Washing machines can start to smell in the summer months if we do not give them a little TLC. When you empty your washing machine, leave the door open for half an hour to allow the drum to dry out. Closing the door straight away will cause it to smell and create mould build-up.

* Leave the detergent drawer slightly open too, and once a week take out the drawer and give it a rinse to flush out the product that gets stuck in there.

Stop smelly shoes

Pop a few unused tea bags inside your smelly shoes to fight off the odours that are caused by heat and bacteria. Tea bags are super absorbent and will suck the moisture and smell right out.

★

Natural mosquito repellent

If it gets hot, we tend to get mosquitos and other insect pests such as horse flies. We all know being bitten is uncomfortable and sometimes painful. In addition to the outdoor citronella candles you can buy, there are a few simple hacks you can employ with ingredients you already have at home.

Option 1

Insects hate the smell of citrus. You can stop them coming into your home by lightly spraying a homemade insect repellent around the entrances.

* Water

* Lemon or lime juice

Add 10ml of the lemon or lime juice to 250ml of water. Shake and then spray around your windows and doors.

Option 2

When you're summer food shopping, chuck in a few juicy limes a week.

* 2–3 limes

* Jar of whole cloves

Halve these and add a few whole cloves by pressing them into the flesh of the lime. When you are entertaining or enjoying time outside, place these around your food table to warn off bugs.

Option 3

This is the one I tend to use the most because I'm a coffee drinker and it is stocked in my cupboard without fail. If you are having a BBQ, this option is simple and effective.

* 2 tbsp of unused coffee grounds

* 1 drop lighter fluid

* Tea towel

Add coffee grounds to a small plate and add a drop of lighter fluid to them. With great care, light the fluid and when it starts to burn, cover the plate with an old wet tea towel. The coffee will start to smoke, which keeps pests at bay.

If you are unlucky enough to be bitten or stung, soothe that pain and stop the irritation by rubbing a small amount of toothpaste over the area.

School summer holidays

The school summer holidays with kids usually mean one thing: a messy house (and corresponding dirty children). Kids' fingerprints and mud are everywhere, chocolate wrappers are left on the floor, grass stains are on their clothes, toys are everywhere collecting dust, and your garden is full of their friends going from outdoors into the house and forgetting to take their shoes off.

So how can you and your home survive the summer holidays? It's not too complicated to keep a well-tidied home over the sumer months, but it does take a little planning and swift action.

* Before the summer holidays even start, get rid of anything you don't need or haven't used in the last year. Keep any clutter to a real minimum, so it doesn't build up to an unconquerable pile over the holidays.

* Summer is the season for parks, lakes, pool days and the beach. Plan days out – it can be as simple as meeting friends at the local park – because by getting out and about, you will save your home the mess and hopefully burn off the children's energy.

★

Plan of action

* A little extra planning can lay the groundwork for a more stress-free summer. Use my Summer Holiday Calendar to plan possible activities and places to go. This way, you're prepared whenever the need for entertainment outside the house arises.

* Once school has finished, put up your Summer Holiday Calendar somewhere everyone can see it. Feel free to add in some unstructured days to allow for flexibility, but do try and maintain as much of your usual routine as possible over the holidays. Keeping a semblance of school-year habits can make the transition back much easier.

Summer Holiday Calendar
July

1	2	3	4
5	6	7	8
9	10	11	12
13	14	15	16
17	18	19	20
21	22	23	24
25	26	27	28
	29	30	31

August

1	2	3	4
5	6	7	8
9	10	11	12
13	14	15	16
17	18	19	20
21	22	23	24
25	26	27	28
29	30	31	

BBQ Checklist

- ☐ Arrange seating
- ☐ Table cloths
- ☐ Plates
- ☐ Glasses
- ☐ Napkins
- ☐ BBQ sauces
- ☐ Bin bags
- ☐ Playlist
- ☐ Decorations such as fairy lights and candles
- ☐ Check outside lighting works if it's a late BBQ
- ☐ Alert neighbours if you could be noisy

BBQ grilling essentials

- ☐ Tin foil
- ☐ Old towel/rags
- ☐ Apron to protect clothes
- ☐ Gas or charcoal
- ☐ Oil
- ☐ BBQ utensils – tongs, spatula, fork
- ☐ Have a separate cooking grill for vegetarians and vegans

Drinks

- ☐ Arrange somewhere to keep drinks cool – big buckets of ice, cool boxes or an empty fridge
- ☐ Bottle openers
- ☐ Corkscrew
- ☐ Alcoholic drinks
- ☐ Soft drinks
- ☐ Drinks for children
- ☐ Glasses
- ☐ Jugs

Food

- ☐ Rolls, hot dogs and burgers
- ☐ Salads: potato salad, couscous, pasta dishes
- ☐ Veggie skewers
- ☐ Meats
- ☐ Vegetarian options
- ☐ Baking potatoes
- ☐ BBQ sauces
- ☐ Cheese slices
- ☐ Coleslaw
- ☐ Desserts

★

Get the kids involved in the housework

As you do throughout the rest of the year, remind your children that taking care of the home you share is a team effort and they must do their bit.

* Simple tasks like putting dirty clothes in the laundry basket, keeping their bedrooms neat, tidying away any toys that are downstairs and running the vacuum around will get them up and out of their beds. Small jobs like this can help take the pressure off you. If your children are old enough, they can empty the dishwasher and do the washing up.

* Create a rota with an incentive scheme tailored to your kids. Encouraging them to help you with the housework is not a bad thing. It will increase their confidence and make them feel proud of their achievements.

* Throughout the holidays, always tackle the smaller jobs before they turn into bigger ones: vacuum up the crumbs before they get spread around, do a daily wash and generally just act as soon as you need to. The worst thing you can do is wait and do a big clean at the end of the week. This ends up turning into a much bigger job, which could take you hours and leave you exhausted.

★

Make some practical, simple and inexpensive changes

* Invest in a large good-quality doormat to stop dirt coming in and serve as a reminder to take off shoes. Further inside the house, place washable rugs in high-traffic areas to help protect the floors and carpets.

* If your children have friends coming around, put a large plastic tub or empty laundry basket by the entrance. As they enter, they can remove their shoes and pop them straight into the tub.

* Keep hand sanitizer by the doors, too, so children can quickly clean their hands before they come in.

* Organize the coat and shoe cupboard. Keep raincoats, boots and light

jackets on hand to prepare for those summer storms. If you don't have a cupboard, create a space by the door. Keep slip-on shoes to hand and sun cream visible so you don't forget to wear it.

* Also invest in some storage containers with lids so at the end of the day toys can be neatly put away with the lid on and then this can go under a bed or in a cupboard.

* Keep to eating in the kitchen or dining room so that you aren't chasing crumbs around the house.

* Cook on the BBQ and eat outside on nice days to keep the dirt out.

* Use disposable plates and cups when the children have friends around.

* Do your food shopping online to save yourself the time and effort of a trip to the supermarket with children in tow.

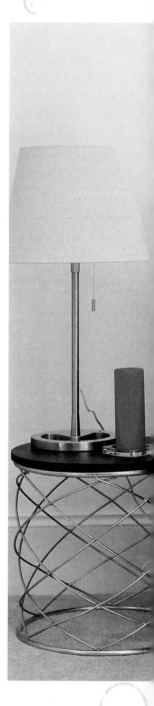

★

Rainy days

* On a rainy day, put a large throw on the sofa and cuddle up to a film with some tasty treats. The throw can be shaken outside and put in the wash to easily save any sticky fingers on the sofa.

* If you face several rainy days in a row, try to arrange to go to other people's homes rather than have everyone at your home – or at least take it in turns.

Keeping your home cool

The summer heat can be lovely, but for some of us, particularly at night time, it can be quite uncomfortable. Sometimes, having a warm house can become a real challenge.

There are a few simple tips and tricks you can employ to keep your family cool without the need for air conditioning.

★

Summer heat hacks

* Step away from the stove and put the slow cooker away – summer is not the time for a hot kitchen with casseroles bubbling away. Switch heavy winter meals for summery salads and BBQs.

* Avoid hot showers and baths – the steam will linger and add to the heat.

* Ditch that thick duvet and go for a much lower tog, or just use a cotton sheet.

* If you have a hot water bottle for the cold winter months, switch it around for the summer: fill with cold water and then pop in the freezer half an hour before bed.

* When trying to sleep, do not charge your phone or any other devices right near your bed, as these radiate heat.

* Close blinds and curtains from early afternoon onward to keep your upstairs rooms cooler.

* Leave your loft hatch slightly open – heat rises, and it will now have another means of escape.

* When you open your windows after sunset, do so on the opposite side of your house so that the air really blows through.

* Fans help beat the heat, but when it's really hot, they do just push hot air around your home. Be strategic and turn your fan around so that it faces the window and pushes the hot air to the window. Another tip for your fan is to place a cold wet tea towel over it.

* Stick to natural light where possible. Light bulbs, as little as they are, give off heat. Switch them off and rely on the sunshine – this will cut your down your energy bills too.

* Add a few houseplants to the front of your sunny windows. The plants absorb some of the sun's energy that would otherwise heat up your home.

* Add a water feature to your garden. Even a small one can create a cooling effect.

* Wear loose and natural fabrics like linen, cotton or Tencel™.

Looking after outdoor furniture

With brighter, sunnier days and bank holidays just around the corner, you'll no doubt be thinking of spending some time outside and dusting down the BBQ. Over the summer months, the outside becomes the new indoors.

Your outdoor or garden furniture is going to endure a lot of wear and tear, so make a point of giving it a little clean. Using a brush, knock off any cobwebs and sweep away any debris. Using a handheld vacuum, pick up the dust and debris from cushions, and then move onto the frame.

Not all outdoor furniture is the same, so you need to make sure you clean the frame that you have correctly.

★

Plastic

No one likes the look of dirty, unsightly plastic garden furniture that has lost its inviting appeal and colour.

* Use warm water and washing-up liquid (or a mild detergent), and wipe down the furniture with a big sponge. Rinse it off with clean water or a hose.

* For any stubborn marks, either use a magic eraser or sprinkle some bicarbonate of soda directly onto a sponge and rub in a circular motion to remove the stains.

* Once the furniture is dry, rub WD-40 all over it if you want a good shine.

★

Metal

* One of the biggest problems with metal furniture is the rusting. When cleaning metal, avoid using harsh chemicals that contain ammonia, and stick to using warm water with a squirt of washing-up liquid. Wash and dry frequently to preserve.

* Metal furniture left outside all year is going to get some rust damage. Don't panic – with a little elbow grease, it will soon vanish. Use some of your household staples to remove: scrunch up some tin foil and use with white wine vinegar and warm soapy water, or buy a special rust-remover product. Removing rust takes some patience, but with persistence it will disappear.

Wood

Wooden garden furniture can be so elegant and fitting to its natural surroundings, but it requires upkeep to keep it looking pristine.

* Using a hard scrubbing brush, knock off any cobwebs and debris and then use a warm sugar-soap solution to wash all over. If you have any stubborn marks, leave the sugar soap on for a few minutes and then shift them with the scrubbing brush. Rinse with a bucket of clean water or a hose and leave to dry.

* Avoid putting any oil on new oak furniture. Oils tend to make the wood go black and pick up dirt.

Rattan

* Brush off any debris and soil, or use a handheld vacuum.

* Take the cushions off and use a lint roller to pick up any awkward bits such as pet hair. Then, use a brush-headed upholstery cleaner to brighten the cushions up. Work up and down in strips so you are not left with any water or soak marks.

* For any annoying bits of debris that get stuck in the rattan, use a cocktail stick to poke them out.

* Use warm soapy water and rinse with clean water or a hose.

* Let the rattan furniture dry naturally in the sun and then pop the cushions back on.

Picnic Checklist

- [ ] Picnic blanket
- [ ] Picnic chairs
- [ ] Cool box
- [ ] Bag so you can take your rubbish away with you
- [ ] Plates
- [ ] Cups
- [ ] Cutlery
- [ ] A sharp knife, if needed
- [ ] Napkins
- [ ] Hand sanitizer
- [ ] If you are taking a bottle of wine or bottles of beer, ensure you have a corkscrew or bottle opener
- [ ] Use containers with lids for salads and sandwiches to prevent them from getting crushed on the journey
- [ ] Cut up fruit for your fruit salad at home so it's ready to go upon arrival
- [ ] Don't forget to take a few outdoor games
- [ ] Remember to place your cool box in the shade rather than leaving it out in direct sunlight
- [ ] Avoid taking mayonnaise, as this can go off in the sun
- [ ] Keep it relatively simple for ease
- [ ] Basic food ideas
- [ ] Sandwiches (stick to classics such as egg, cheese and pickle, and ham and English mustard)
- [ ] Small sausage rolls
- [ ] Quiches
- [ ] Cocktail sausages
- [ ] Cheeses
- [ ] Scotch eggs
- [ ] Green salad
- [ ] Bread sticks
- [ ] Veg sticks of carrot, pepper and cucumber with dips
- [ ] Olives
- [ ] Fruit salad (watermelon cut into chunks, strawberries and grapes are simple to prep)
- [ ] Fairy cakes
- [ ] Crisps

Picnic perfection

I used to love taking my three children to the park and having a picnic. It was an inexpensive day out and something we all enjoyed, especially if were meeting up with friends and having a giant get-together.

A good picnic is not just about the food, but also about the weather and presentation. It does need a little planning – you don't want to rock up, picnic ready, and suddenly realize you have forgotten the plates or cups or that your cool box is leaking. Before you set off, make sure your Tupperware lids are on tight!

Once you have prepped your picnic, you can look forward to truly sitting back and enjoying the surroundings.

Follow my simple Picnic Checklist, and you'll be good to go.

Holiday prep

It's that time of the year when we all start going off on our holidays. Whether we're camping or sunning ourselves on a beach, there is a lot of preparation that needs to be done. Realistically, we can't simply get up and go.

A good few weeks before you leave, you need to start your holiday preparation.

★

Beauty and personal care

* Get any beauty appointments booked for a few days before you travel. Wintry feet may need a little TLC and a lick of paint, or you may want to fit in haircuts for the kids.

★

Preparations for your pets

* Make sure you arrange pet care with someone or somewhere you trust. Guinea pigs and rabbits need feeding and their water changing. Find a trustworthy friend or neighbour to help you with this.

* For your cat or dog, use a local cattery or kennels. Do your research – read reviews or ask friends what their recommendations are. You want to make sure you leave your pet happy and comfortable.

* If you go on holiday in your own country and decide to take your pet away for the first time, take along their usual bedding and favourite toys – your pet needs to feel just as comfortable as you, and a new environment will be strange for them.

* Remember that not all accommodation allows pets; be sure to check this out when making your booking.

* Travel safely with your pet by using a pet seat belt or a crate in the boot.

My top tips for holidays

* Create a master packing checklist. Use your checklist whenever you go away, even if it's just for a few nights. This way, you can avoid forgetting anything. Once items are packed, they're ticked off, and the list comes with you to pack for your return.

* Save bag space for any holiday purchases.

* Check the weather and pack accordingly.

* Take small reusable travel bottles for your washing detergent (for hand-washing of clothes), washing-up liquid and a multipurpose spray. As you can imagine, I do bring a few cleaning products from home, but I tend to go straight to a supermarket upon arrival and grab my essentials. Plus, I love to check out the local cleaning products. Use travel bottles for beauty items, too – it saves you having to take half the bathroom with you.

* Pack a waterproof bag for your damp swimsuit, so you don't soak everything else in your case on your way home.

* What's the first thing everyone wants to do when they arrive? Go to the beach or pool and start the holiday! Pack your towel and swimwear last, giving you a quick turnaround from landing to lounger. The towel will also cushion and protect the rest of the items in your case.

* Take a small hand-held steamer with you to banish the creases from packed clothes. Steamers are also great for refreshing clothes mid-holiday.

* Other than my essential travel documents and iPad, I also take a set of lightweight clothes for each of us in my hand luggage. If your luggage is lost or you are heavily delayed and end up spending a night at an airport hotel, you'll be able to change.

* Limit liquids in hand luggage and pop your valuables in to keep them close to you at all times. Of course, I keep cleaning wipes in there so I can freshen up my tray table on the aircraft and keep my hands clean.

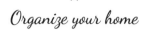

Organize your home

While you're away, your home is going to be sitting empty for some time, so a few things need to be put into place.

* If you have neighbours, ask them if they could come and put out your dustbins and water the plants, and offer to do the same for them if they go away. You don't need to be too friendly with your neighbours to ask for small gestures like this; it is a neighbourly thing to offer each other and reassures you that your home is being looked after.

* Don't leave your home looking unoccupied, but do leave it secure. Double- and triple-check doors and windows and keep any valuables in a safe place.

* Try not to tell everyone you are going on holiday and don't announce on social media that you are all away.

* Make sure you have cancelled any food and newspaper deliveries.

* It's a good idea to invest in some automatic timers for a few lights that you can programme to come on at night. Leave the curtains and blinds open – nothing reveals that a house is unoccupied as much as curtains drawn during the day.

* Make sure to mow the lawn before you go so you don't come back to a totally overgrown meadow.

Organize your travel documents

Papers, papers everywhere. One of the more challenging aspects of travelling is the collection of documents and critical items that you must keep organized and available at all times during your holiday.

* Upon booking your family holiday, check the expiry dates of your passports so you have time to renew if necessary.

* Don't leave the task of getting local currency for your destination to the last minute. The cheapest rates are always to be found online.

* In your hand luggage, put a travel wallet that holds your driving licence, boarding passes, passports, hotel and car hire information – all in the order in which you will need them. Write down emergency contact numbers in case you lose your phone. These days, how many of us actually remember a phone number? You should also write down your passport number(s) and keep them safe with a copy each in your checked suitcase and hand luggage.

* It's good practice to back up your medical information. If you take any prescription medications, get a letter from your doctor explaining what you take and why.

* Whatever means of organization you choose to employ, make sure you do something. The last thing you want on a restful holiday is to become stressed because you've lost an important travel document.

★

Don't leave the packing to the last minute

Never leave packing to the last minute: it will only stress you out and get your holiday off on the wrong foot. Start to think about packing a good week in advance. Use a clothes rail and put this up in a spare room or one of your bedrooms and start to plan your outfits – this way, you won't wear them again before you leave.

* Try and pack like a minimalist: choose outfits that can be can dressed up and down, and which you know are easy to style and accessorize.

* Choose versatile accessories. Think day-to-night shoes, a stunning necklace and a belt that will go with everything.

* Don't overpack. We have all loaded our cases with endless pairs of shorts and ended up wearing only a few pairs. Be ruthless – lay all of your clothes on your bed and then aim to reduce them by a third. Always leave some breathing room for any holiday souvenirs you might bring back.

* Vacuum packs are fantastic, and you don't actually need a vacuum. All you need to do is roll the air out. They keep your clothes neatly packed together and will protect clothes from any spillages. The disadvantage of using vacuum packs is that your clothes may get a little creased. Vacuum packs can tear, so it's worth spending money and getting durable ones.

* Be aware that your clothes will still weigh the same when vacuum-packed. You may have filled your case with more than your normal amount, so don't forget to weigh your case before you go and keep it below the luggage weight your airlines allows. Do this using digital scales, and bring them with you for the journey home – dirty washing does weigh more than clean.

* Another tool that allows you to keep items together neatly is packing cubes. I find these particularly helpful for accessories, lotions and potions. When you arrive at your destination, they make it easy to know where everything is. If you have all your underwear in one cube, you can simply lift this and pop it straight in a drawer rather than fully unpacking. The cubes help prevent overpacking and keep belongings tidy even in transit.

Pre-holiday Checklist

- Clean the fridge and chuck out or freeze any food that will go off while you're away
- Make sure the washing machine and tumble dryer are empty
- Ensure all windows are closed
- Print travel documents, e-tickets and voucher deals

- Empty all bins and clean them out
- Mow the lawn
- Leave bleach in the bottom of all the toilets

- Tell your neighbours you are away and ask them to keep an eye on your home (e.g. put the bins out)
- Leave a spare key with a trusted person

- Set out-of-office emails
- Unplug computers
- Turn off appliances
- Turn off gas
- Water houseplants
- Set timers on some lights
- Adjust the thermostat
- Set security alarm
- Lock house, garage and garden gate

- If you have pets, organize someone to look after them

- Ensure you have cash with you for emergencies
- Destination weather check to ensure you have packed correctly

Holiday Packing Checklist

Hand luggage

- [ ] Passports
- [ ] Tickets
- [ ] Purse/wallet
- [ ] Currency/travellers' cheques/credit card
- [ ] Hotel/transfer/car hire information

- [ ] Tissues
- [ ] Wet wipes
- [ ] Hand sanitizer
- [ ] Chewing gum
- [ ] Small perfume/body spray
- [ ] Facial moisturizer
- [ ] Spare underwear
- [ ] Entertainment
- [ ] Boiled sweets

Clothing and accessories

- [ ] Underwear
- [ ] Socks
- [ ] PJs
- [ ] Swimwear
- [ ] T-shirts/tops
- [ ] Shorts/skirts/dresses

- [ ] Jeans/long trousers
- [ ] Eveningwear
- [ ] Evening bag
- [ ] Hoodie/jumper
- [ ] Lightweight jacket
- [ ] Trainers
- [ ] Shoes
- [ ] Flip-flops
- [ ] Hat
- [ ] Sunglasses
- [ ] Accessories
- [ ] Beach towels

Personal bits

- [ ] Skincare
- [ ] Deodorant
- [ ] Toothbrush/toothpaste
- [ ] Hairbrush/comb
- [ ] Hairdryer/straighteners/tongs
- [ ] Shampoo/conditioner

- [ ] Sun cream
- [ ] After sun/aloe vera gel
- [ ] Perfume/aftershave
- [ ] Shower gel
- [ ] Razor
- [ ] Plasters
- [ ] Paracetamol/Calpol
- [ ] Antiseptic
- [ ] Insect repellent

Extras

- [ ] Camera
- [ ] Travel plugs
- [ ] Reusable water bottle/ coffee cup
- [ ] Bedding/pillowcases
- [ ] Multipurpose spray
- [ ] Cleaning wipes
- [ ] Travel-sized detergent
- [ ] Air fresheners
- [ ] Tea towel
- [ ] Dish cloth
- [ ] Mug
- [ ] Paper cups
- [ ] Bin bags
- [ ] Toilet roll

Holiday return

Coming home from holiday and being chucked right into the deep end has happened to us all, but it can be avoided. There are a few things you can do to make your return easier and less stressful.

★

Make sure your laundry is up to date

* There is no better feeling than an empty laundry basket and a non-existent ironing pile. This can be rare for busy families, but challenge yourself before you go away to ensure you are up to date. You are going to be coming home with a big pile of washing and ironing, and you really do not need to add to this pile. If you're struggling for time, there is no harm in using the launderette or a local ironing service.

* You may be coming home right before the children go back to school, so you need to make sure all their uniforms, stationery and bags are ready.

★

Food delivery

* If you have a regular food delivery, organize this before you go. You won't want to go to the supermarket and do a full weekly shop.

* Alternatively, ask a friend or neighbour to drop fresh milk and bread into your home just before you return, so you can at least have a cup of tea if you haven't got much else in.

★

Plan a meal

Cook up a healthy meal and pop it in the freezer before you go so you can defrost and enjoy when you get home. Holidays normally mean overeating and not eating so well. You may be craving a home-cooked healthy dinner. Knock up a quick Bolognese or a soup packed with vegetables to dig into.

★

Don't jump straight into socializing

Give yourself a few days before you start to go out with friends again, and try not to host any gatherings at your house. Ease yourself back in gently.

★

Back to work

If you have the flexibility, book an extra day into your diary following the end of your holiday to give yourself time to adjust. It can be trying to come home in the early hours of the morning and then have to be at work by 9am. Use your out-of-office email notification to your advantage: don't switch it off until you have caught up.

Summer To-do List

Priority tasks

Texts and emails to send

Shopping list (food and household essentials)

Phone calls to make

Cleaning tasks

What's for tea?

NOTES

Autumn

Now that the days are getting shorter, the nights longer and the temperature outside is slowly dropping, it's time to think about your autumn clean. Organize to get ready for those cold winter months when we spend much more time indoors cooking homely meals, playing family games and watching TV by the fireplace.

You don't always have to follow a checklist or schedule, but it is good to spend a few moments at the end of the chapter evaluating your home and what you feel you need to get done.

We all talk about the big "spring clean", but personally, I feel the autumn clean is just as important. Doing an autumn clean will update the home and prepare you for winter.

A few things you want to include in your autumn clean are preparing the entrance areas with good heavy doormats, checking the batteries in smoke detectors, checking that light bulbs work and sealing up those draughty areas where the cold can easily get in and have an impact on your heating bill.

One of my top tips is to bring the outside in – so now is the time to change over the summer scatter cushions, throws and candles and bring in the more autumnal ones. This is so much cheaper than a room makeover, but it gives you something different to look at and will make you feel in season, a bit like the way we are with our wardrobe – we stop wearing the strappy summer dresses and sandals and we get out the big comfortable jumpers and boots.

Autumn checks & hacks

The beginning of autumn is the ideal time to get your home looking great so you can enjoy your surroundings with a cozy night in, come rain or shine. Halloween and the festive season are fast approaching and chances are that you will do some party hosting or have unexpected visitors popping in. Make it easier by preparing the house, and yourself, ahead of time.

★

Medicine cabinet clear-out

Clearing out the medicine cabinet should be one of the first items on your autumn to-do list. First, take everything out and take stock. Check all the bottles and boxes and remove any that are empty – there are bound to be one or two – and then check all the expiry dates. Stock up on cold and flu remedies, vitamins and nasal drops. If anyone in your home takes regular medication, make sure you have enough of a supply and refills are arranged.

★

Keep healthy

Ensure that you buy lots of fresh fruit every week. Not only are they good for you, but seasonal fruits such as apples, pears, berries and satsumas in bowls bring lovely colours indoors and create a pleasing environment. Little bowls of nuts also do the same, and are a smart snack choice for energy.

★

Use natural elements

Take a trip to the woods and pick up pine cones, which come in all shapes and sizes and can look really lovely in a ceramic bowl or vase, as a cheap way to bring autumn indoors.

* You can also combine candles with pumpkins and fruits and arrange in a simple wooden box or crate to create a lovely seasonal display.

Warm up your rooms

A quick way to add warmth and texture to your room without replacing furniture or your colour scheme is to change up your soft furnishings.

* Look at switching your throws, cushions and curtains to give a more autumnal feel. In the kitchen or dining room, set your tables with warmer colours like red and ochre. Store your spring/summer items for next year.

* Add in a few diffusers and candles along with some little autumn-inspired ornaments like mini pumpkins. Candlelight always makes your home feel warm and cozy. See page 147 for tips on candle safety.

Last chance for small renovations

The first autumn weeks are the best time to fix those niggling issues.

* Check that your fence will get you through the winter winds, and fill in any cracks in walls to prevent those spiders coming in.

* Freshen up painted walls if needed – the hallway tends to take the biggest battering in the home. Remove any marks that you can, and if you can get away with just touching up the paintwork, do this rather than embarking on a big paint job.

Put away patio and garden furniture

During winter, you won't be needing your garden furniture. Moreover, cold and wet weather can deteriorate it. Take advantage of the last warm days of the summer, and rinse everything outside with warm soapy water. Dry and store the furniture in your garage or cover it with outdoor furniture covers. This also applies for gardening equipment and children's toys, as well as for the barbecue. Try not to leave anything out and uncovered, or it may rust.

★

Get started gardening

If you want your garden to bloom with colour next spring, you want to get bulbs in for your tulips, snowdrops and daffodils now, before the first big frost hits. Spring bulbs require time for their roots to develop before the cold sets in properly, so set aside some time and get digging.

★

Clear those cobwebs

It's spider season! That means one thing for your walls, ceilings and any other crevices that these eight-legged creatures can possibly find their way into: an endless amount of those annoying, unsightly cobwebs.

* Make a point of grabbing a long duster weekly, going all the way up to the ceiling. Focus on corners, around the light fittings, and sweep over the walls themselves as well. They somehow manage to get everywhere!

★

Watch your window frames

Get your windows sparkling this season! As you start to turn the heating dials up and the radiators begin throwing out warmth, condensation will start to appear around the windows.

* It's important to keep your windows and frames clean to stop mould and mildew build-up. If your windows have bad condensation and you wake up to damp on the inside frames, make sure to dry them every day.

★

Don't forget to clean out your drains and gutters

All those autumnal leaves may look beautiful on the ground, but they'll cause real problems for your drains and gutters by the middle of the season, so it's a good idea to give them a clear-out to prevent blockage. Pop some gardening gloves on, climb up on a (stable) ladder and empty the gutters of leaf and debris build-up.

Let's go back to school!

As the summer holidays draw to a close, it's back to school we go. Over the holidays, many of us have lost our regular routines and it is now time to kick-start them again. With a little forward planning, the transition from holiday mode to term-time organization can be made a lot easier.

A few days before the first day back, reset your family's sleep and eating routines. It's important your child maintains a high level of energy when starting back, as getting back into the school routine can be exhausting.

★

Calendars, cooking and colour-coding

When kids go back to school, they come home with a list of important dates for the next school year which include mufti days, sports days and school discos – not forgetting the dreaded school-photograph days.

* Get these dates written down on the family planner (in a different colour for each family member) and in your phone, and share with the family. You don't want your child turning up in school uniform on a non-uniform day. As a parent, it's horrible to feel as though you have let your child down.

* On top of these dates, there are also school trips, so follow the payment plans and get these dates added to your calendar too. You don't want to be the parent that the school have to chase for money on a regular basis.

* To make all the paperwork easier, create a system of folders and keep them somewhere safe. You can also keep any special achievement certificates, as well as artwork and reports, in these personalized folders. Then, at the end of the school year, you can scan everything into the computer so that it is all saved – and not left hanging on the fridge for the next five years.

* Make sure you implement a family meal planner (see pages 14–15) to help you cope with the busier days. Meal planning not only saves you time – it also saves you money by eliminating food waste.

Pack a punch with your packed lunch

School meals aren't everyone's idea of a good lunch, although they have come a long way over the years. If you prefer to make your own, I have put together a few simple ideas to help add variety to packed lunches. I like to keep mine colourful to keep them interesting, too.

Sandwich swap

* Tuna pasta: sweetcorn, mayo, wholemeal pasta and tuna, served cold.

* Fried rice with spring onions, soy sauce and bacon, served cold.

* Cheese and apple: grate hard cheese and an apple, add a drop of lemon and mayo for a cracker topping.

Snack ideas

Use snack pots to add healthy variety to a packed lunch. Prepare and label one for each day of the week and leave them in the fridge so you can grab and go on the busy midweek mornings.

* Carrot and cucumber sticks with hummus

* Fruit salad

* Fruit kebab

* Popcorn

* Olives

* Crackers

* Sultanas

* Pumpkin seeds

* Yogurt drops

* Homemade flapjacks

Getting younger children organized in the morning before school

If you have younger children, create a Getting Ready for School Checklist and leave it in their bedrooms so you don't have to keep asking them to do things in the morning rush. I found that this really helped me when mine were younger, as they used to be proud that they had finished their list of morning jobs to do. Mine included some basics:

* Come down for breakfast

* Brush teeth and have a wash

* Get dressed

* Put PJs away and tidy up

* Pack school bag

* Don't forget your lunch box

* Shoes and coat by 8.20am

To protect school shoes from puddles, spray them with WD-40.

Small lists or charts like this can really help take the strain off when you're under time pressure, so it's definitely something I recommend you try. Maybe also introduce a little reward at the end of the month.

★

Suited and booted: uniforms

Label up all the school uniforms. To make it less of a chore, use iron-on or washable stick-on labels, not the ones you have to sew into garments.

If you're a busy family, make sure you have five sets of school uniforms per child so that if you don't get time to do washing in the week, you know that your child will be going into school looking neat and smart.

Back-to-School Checklist

Stationery

- [ ] Pencils
- [ ] Pencil sharpener
- [ ] Coloured pencils
- [ ] Eraser
- [ ] Glue stick
- [ ] Ruler
- [ ] Pencil case
- [ ] Calculator
- [ ] Geometry set
- [ ] Highlighters
- [ ] Lined notepad
- [ ] Drawing pad
- [ ] Post-it notes
- [ ] Folders

Outerwear

- [ ] Trainers
- [ ] School shoes
- [ ] Winter coat
- [ ] Raincoat
- [ ] Gloves
- [ ] Scarf
- [ ] Small umbrella
- [ ] Rucksack
- [ ] Book bag

Lunch

- [ ] Lunch box
- [ ] Water bottle
- [ ] Hand wipes/sanitizer

Uniform

- [ ] Shirts/polos
- [ ] Tie
- [ ] Jumpers/cardigans
- [ ] Blazer
- [ ] Socks
- [ ] Tights
- [ ] PE kit
- [ ] PE hoodie
- [ ] PE bag
- [ ] Swimming kit

For parents

- [ ] Clothes labels
- [ ] Permanent marker
- [ ] Calendar/diary
- [ ] School contact details

★

Tackling homework

While their homework is their own responsibility, look into and suggest a few educational apps for your child to download on their tablet or phone for reference, research or learning.

* Plan some time in your routine for homework support, even if it's just 30 minutes a week, and dedicate this time to your child without any distractions. Encourage your child to do their homework downstairs and not in their rooms, to encourage focus and productivity. I create a little homework station where they can find everything they need, from stationery to a clear workspace.

* Try to keep your school routine consistent so that everyone in the house follows it. A few days of leaving at a set time and knowing when homework time begins is all it takes for the routine to become the norm. If it helps streamline your schedule, make packed lunches the night before and have your children hang their school uniform up in bedrooms, with polished shoes by the door ready to go.

★

And finally...

* Don't forget, your five-minute cleaning challenge is easily doable in the morning before the school run. You don't need to do every room, but set yourself a goal to do at least two rooms, which is just 10 minutes of housework. Set your timer and go, go, go.

* Going back to school can be stressful for kids. Remind them that everything will be okay and that they can count on you being there for them, no matter what. Knowing that they are loved and supported will keep most of the back-to-school jitters away. Best of luck in the coming school year!

Student tips and cleaning

Sending a young adult off to university is a substantial change for both parties. While they face new living conditions and experiences, you must decide if or how to maintain your child's bedroom and belongings that are not with them at university. The tips and advice that follow are for students, so have your child read these as they begin their preparations to move away.

Surviving student living takes a lot of patience and teamwork. When you first move into shared accommodation, you are going to be hit with the reality of sharing your personal space with complete strangers for an entire year. You'll need to stock up on essentials before you fly the nest – use my Student Essentials Checklist for ideas on useful items to take.

Student living is all about working together and supporting each other. The best way to tackle it is to set the standard as soon as you all meet: sit down together and get this boring conversation about chores out of the way as soon as possible. Draw up a list of tasks you think the space needs and see who is best at what task (or who is willing). This might include:

* Shopping for household essentials

* Cleaning

* Cooking

* Washing up

* Managing the bills

Discuss what items you are going to need to maintain your property, including cleaning products. Students do tend to be on a tighter budget, and with that in mind, I've got my list of Cleaning Tips for Students – all are cost-effective and limit the use of chemicals.

Student Essentials Checklist

- [ ] Towels and bath mat
- [ ] Toiletries
- [ ] Toilet roll
- [ ] Flip-flops if sharing a shower area
- [ ] Dressing gown
- [ ] Slippers

- [ ] Bedding – pillows, duvet, covers and mattress and pillow protectors. Include a throw – this is great for protecting bedding when other students want to come and chill in your room.

- [ ] Mirror
- [ ] Clock
- [ ] Coat hangers
- [ ] Clothes rail, if no wardrobe provided
- [ ] Small safe to protect your valuables
- [ ] Scented candles

- [ ] Pictures of home
- [ ] Kitchen utensils
- [ ] Basic cleaning caddy – cloths and sponges, multipurpose cleaner, washing up liquid, toilet bleach, fabric refresher, lint roller, white wine vinegar and spray bottles.

- [ ] Don't forget your bicarb and lemons!
- [ ] Stationery – ring binders, Post-it notes, Blu Tack, student planner, calculator, writing paper and notepads, storage folders and your course textbooks

Cleaning Tips for Students

* Check the discounted aisle in the supermarket for cheaper branded products.

* Grab a bunch of microfibre cloths, as these can be used for nearly all types of cleaning.

* Find a good multipurpose cleaning spray that can be used for nearly any cleaning job.

* Invest in bleach for the toilets – the cheapest bleach in the supermarket will be just as good as the most expensive one.

* Buy plenty of durable bin bags so you can clean up easily after all those student parties.

* If you don't have a vacuum, try to borrow one from a family member to save money. If you have only non-carpeted floors, a good brush will serve just as well.

* A mop and a bucket will be needed for any accidents or spillages, as well as a sanitizing floor clean every so often.

* There may already be some reliable cleaning staples living in your kitchen cupboards. White wine vinegar is a natural cleaner that is fantastic at tackling any mould and mildew patches, and it's also great for streak-free window cleaning. Lemon juice is cheap and removes hard-water marks on your shower screen, stainless-steel draining board or taps.

* If you have any vodka left over from those crazy parties, hold onto it rather than drink those last few drops – vodka can help remove stains on carpets and marks on high-gloss kitchen cabinets.

* Shaving foam is also great for carpet stains and for around the bottom of the toilet bowl, where urine and vomit may have splashed.

* Coke is another product that will clean rust and the built-up limescale you can sometimes get in your toilet.

★

Working together

Who is going to clean the bathroom or kitchen? Who is going to replace the toilet roll? Cleaning is unlikely to be volunteered for, so make a pact that each tenant is responsible for their own space, but the shared areas need TLC from everyone. Dirty dishes have a tendency to pile up quickly in a student house. You have two options to discuss with your housemates here.

* Option one is to do your own dishes as you use them and then put them away, as dirty washing-up crowding the sink won't make you very popular. Tidy up books and magazines you have been reading in shared areas, stick to doing your own laundry and if you make a mess, clean it up.

* Option two is to create a rota. It doesn't have to be too intense, but should be enough to keep your shared areas clean and tidy. Everyone's standards will be different, so it's going to take a few weeks to strike the perfect balance! Use my Cleaning Rota Template to get started.

Moving out

The year will soon be over and the end of tenancy clean will need to take place. You'll need to give the whole place a thorough deep clean – after all, at the end of your tenancy you're going to want your deposit back.

★

Declutter first

Anything that you don't need or no longer want needs to be disposed of sooner rather than later. With student life, there can be a lot of rubbish, from beer bottles hanging around to pizza boxes hidden under sofas.

* Use a strong bin bag and start to get this rubbish and clutter clear, with the help of your housemates.

Cleaning Rota Template

Monthly tasks

- ☐ Clean the windows
- ☐ Tackle the cobwebs
- ☐ Dust the skirting boards
- ☐ Wipe down the front door

Daily tasks

- ☐ Vacuum
- ☐ Wash up dirty dishes
- ☐ Open the windows for 10 minutes to air the space
- ☐ Plump up sofa cushions
- ☐ Clear plates and mugs left in the shared areas
- ☐ Clean the kitchen sink
- ☐ Bleach the toilets
- ☐ Take out the rubbish and recycling

Weekly tasks

- ☐ Vacuum and mop
- ☐ Full bathroom clean
- ☐ Wipe out the oven (doing this weekly will save you hiring a professional service at the end of the year, saving you money)
- ☐ Clean kitchen surfaces
- ☐ Dust living surfaces

★

...Then tackle the cleaning

* Clear all toiletries from the bathroom and clear out the kitchen cupboards before you start wiping anything down.

* In the bathroom, make sure you remove all limescale and soapy streaks from taps and the shower screen. Using half a lemon dipped in bicarb, rub all over your shower screen. Buff dry with a clean microfibre cloth.

* Get the windows open to give the property a really good airing.

* Focus on doors, handles and mirrors and thoroughly wipe off all smears and stains, and always give the skirting boards a wipe down. It's amazing what a good cloth and warm soapy water will achieve.

* Start at the top of each room and work your way down, tackling those cobwebs and dusty walls. Use a dry mop if you haven't got a long duster, and then rinse this off before you clean the floors.

* Don't forget to move items of furniture to check underneath and behind them.

* Use a good strong oven cleaner for the oven, open the window and go off and do another task to allow the product to work. If the build-up in the oven is really bad, I suggest all going in together to pay for a professional oven-cleaning service.

* Don't forget any outside areas in the frenzy of getting the inside ones perfected. There could be cigarette ends and after-party mess, and even neglected grass and planted areas that need a bit of gardening green fingers. Remember – this scene will be the landlord's first view upon inspection.

These little finishing touches can make a huge difference and ensure you reclaim your deposit and leave the home clean for the next tenants.

Lamps, lights and lampshades

Now that the nights are drawing in, you will start to use your lights and lamps much more often to create that relaxing, cozy atmosphere.

* Lamps and lights can really hold onto dust, especially fabric lampshades. Spend some time going around your home, giving your lamps a dry dust using a microfibre cloth or a feather duster. For shades, use a lint roller rather than a vacuum nozzle, as these will not cause any damage to the shade. Make sure you clean both the inside and the outside of your lampshades.

* If you have grubby hand marks or stains on your shades, delicately rub a soft facewipe over the mark until it has gone. A heavy cloth will cause damage; I find a thin wipe the best solution here. You can also dampen a dryer sheet and use that. The best way to prevent these grubby marks is to keep your shades out of reach of children, but of course that is easier said than done!

* Turn the lights off, let the bulbs cool, then spray some glass cleaner on a microfibre cloth and gently wipe the lightbulb to remove any dust and grime. After a good clean, your light bulbs will really ping.

Always dust first and vacuum afterwards!

Moths

Are you wondering why you keep spotting moths on your bedroom's walls at this time of year? The increase in the clothes moth population has been widely reported, and early autumn is when they are most likely to attack our wardrobe.

Many flying insects are drawn towards light, but moths like to hide away in dark spaces, such as your wardrobes and cupboards.

★

How to prevent moths from coming into your home

One reason moths are drawn to your wardrobe and the clothes within is because they are attracted to smells – in particular, the sweat and oils released by the human body.

* When you are doing your wardrobe transition and storing away your summer clothes, ensure all the clothes are clean and that you store them in an airtight bag rather than a box.

* Make sure you regularly vacuum in your bedroom. If you spot any webbing or cocoons in the corner of your bedroom or even in your wardrobe, make sure you remove these right away. This will be where moths are laying their eggs.

* Keep your wardrobe well ventilated. In order to let the light in and for fresh air to circulate, occasionally leave its door open at the same time as a nearby window.

* You can buy cedar wood coat hangers; these are quite expensive, but if you have a moth problem and your clothes are being ruined, it is more than worth the investment.

* Wipe over your wardrobe doors and windows with a natural solution of water and vinegar.

* Hang small bags of lavender or bay leaves inside your wardrobes or pop some lavender essential oil onto a cotton pad and poke the top of your hanger through. With both of these ideas, your wardrobe will smell fantastic, too. You can also buy natural moth sprays.

* Keep clothes as clean as possible, and try not to put dirty or unwashed clothes back in your wardrobe, as moths are drawn to these.

Energy-saving hacks

Now that we are spending more time indoors, it's helpful to think about the amount of household energy we use. When we save energy, we save money, so try some of these ideas and cut back where you can. Your bank balance and the environment will be grateful for it.

* If you're not in a room, ensure that no lights or lamps are on – and when you are using them, make sure you've got energy-saving bulbs installed.

* Turn your heating thermostat down a notch or two – and monitor your energy consumption by using a smart meter.

* Repair any dripping taps or showerheads. Not only does this waste water, but they could be dripping hot water, which will cost you over time.

* When choosing new appliances for your home, choose highly energy-efficient ones. They may be slightly more expensive, but they will save you money in the long run.

* Wash your clothes at a lower temperature, around 30°.

* To keep draughts out, seal up any cracks in the floor or skirting boards, block any air vents and unused chimneys and line your letterbox.

* Cut your shower time by a minute.

* Close curtains at night to keep the warmth in.

* Throw open the windows to air your home in the mornings, but don't leave them open for long. Always make sure they are shut when the heating is on.

* When you have fully charged your phone and tablet, turn the switch off at the plug and remove your device.

* Cover hard floors with rugs to make them feel warmer on your feet.

* Don't hang clothes on your radiator to dry – this just lowers the temperature of the room and will make your boiler work much harder, which is not good.

Autumn To-do List

Here are a few ideas to get you started on your own Autumn To-do List.

☐ Place draught excluders by doors

☐ Change over the duvets

☐ Flip and turn all your household mattresses

☐ Wash slippers and dressing gowns

☐ Switch candles to autumn and winter fragrances

☐ Change simple decorations such as scatter cushions, throws, and candles

☐ Change your flower displays

☐ Check radiators are working

☐ Test and clean your smoke detectors

☐ Wash your carpets (hire a machine, a cleaning company, or invest in your own carpet cleaner)

☐ Swap doormats for heavier ones that will keep the dirt out

☐ Take down curtains and clean them (dry clean, or if they are washable, pop them in your machine)

☐ Check that light bulbs are working and make sure you have spares

☐ Check fuses

☐ Tidy away garden furniture

☐ Empty dead hanging baskets

☐ Plant bulbs

The perfect Halloween party

As the season (and its attendant weather) marches on, we can't help but think about Christmas. By now, holiday cards will be in the shops and you may have already started buying presents. Halloween is sort of a mini kick-off to get us in the mood for the festive season ahead. Everyone loves dressing up for Halloween, especially the kids!

You don't have to be a professional party planner to host the perfect party. The key is to be organized and have a few fun ideas up your sleeve.

★

Guest list

Who will you invite? Decide, and give them plenty of notice. Life is busy, and people aren't often free with just a few days' notice. If it's a fancy-dress party, specify this on the invite.

★

Be flexible

You don't need to hold your party on 31 October exactly – you can be flexible and do the weekend before or after.

★

Don't do it all

On your invite, ask for guests to please bring something. If they bring a few other drink options or a pudding, this can help make your task a bit easier.

★

Create a menu

Decide on a finger-food menu that caters to everyone's requirements. Keep it simple and colourful and perhaps use a quirky theme. Keep all the food to

one area to eliminate the mess in other rooms and leave a few rubbish bags around for people to scrape their plates into or clean up after themselves.

For a Halloween party menu, you can't go wrong by preparing some of my favourite spooky nibbles in advance.

* Finger sandwiches

* Spiderweb pretzels

* Hotdogs

* Witches' pastry fingers

* Pizza

* White-chocolate dipped strawberry ghosts

* Dipped marshmallows

* Marbled spiderweb cupcakes

Serve "bloody punch"

An easy way to serve drinks at your party is to create a punch. You can use raspberry squash and lemonade to create a "bloody punch" to match your snacks. Put some fake vampire teeth on the ladle as an easy way to decorate and add to the fun, or put eyeball sweets on the rims of your serving glasses.

Make a shopping list

A solid shopping list helps ensure that you get enough of each ingredient and enough food to feed your guests. Pick up a few frozen snacks so you have a back-up in case your homemade food goes wrong.

Music

Every party needs music! Prepare your playlist and make sure it lasts for the duration of the party so no songs repeat. Your playlist of Halloween-themed music can be as traditional as "Thriller" and "Monster Mash", or can be based on musical soundtracks like *The Phantom of the Opera*. Have a few sound effects up your sleeve; a well-placed scream can make the night and make your guests jump.

★

Decorations

Make your Halloween decorations with the kids – go to town with festive colours such as black, orange and red.

* Organize balloons, paper chains, tablecloths, mini pumpkins and candles. Create an even spookier atmosphere with a few lanterns and fairy lights and add spooky decorations to the front door.

* Set an eerie mood by switching your normal lightbulbs for coloured bulbs or black lights.

★

Halloween games

Incorporating games into the evening is a great way to involve guests in conversation and encourage new friendships. Make sure to organize it beforehand and have concise directions; nothing kills a party game faster than a confused and bored guest.

★

Don't forget the trick-or-treaters

If you are hosting something at home on Halloween itself, you don't want to ignore the doorbell. Since your house is decorated and the lights are on, people will assume that you are offering treats. Appoint a few of the children at the party to help hand out the sweets – or leave a cute sign by a basket or cauldron full of treats that says, "Excuse our absence, ghoulish party underway. Please help yourself to one treat!"

★

Relax and have fun

It's your party and you should enjoy it as much as your guests!

Autumn To-do List

Priority tasks

....
....
....
....
....
....
....
....
....
....
....
....

Texts and emails to send

....
....
....
....
....
....
....
....
....
....
....
....
....

Shopping list (food and household essentials)

....
....
....
....
....
....
....

Phone calls to make

Cleaning tasks

What's for tea?

NOTES

Winter

I adore the winter. I love nothing better than cozy nights in with the candles burning; it's such a lovely feeling. But because we spend more time indoors over the winter, we need to be even more on top of the cleaning and making our home a more comfortable and enjoyable place to spend time.

At the start of winter, the bright autumn colours are still there when we look outside the window, but these will soon disappear, to be replaced with the bleak winterscape. Making your home colourful and cozy keeps your mood lifted and makes you eager to return home after a long cold day.

Winter is a good time to really get stuck into organizing and de-cluttering. With the New Year approaching, you want to be thinking, "Out with the old and in with the new"!

Winter cleaning tips

★

Defend your floors

One of the most important tasks to do over the winter is to prepare your entrances for the winter months ahead. Winter brings with it mud and snow, and this is easily brought into your home if you are not prepared.

* Pop doormats outside so you can wipe your shoes before entering. This should prevent muck such as twigs, leaves and lumps of mud coming in.

* Have another mat indoors to allow you a space to take off your shoes. Give this mat a good shake outside every few days.

* Keep the inside entrance dry with a simple umbrella holder. The rain and snow of winter keep umbrellas in constant use, so give them somewhere to dry off that is easily accessible for you.

★

Gloves, hats and scarves

* Pair up gloves and stack them neatly where they can be easily accessed without falling into a jumble again; single gloves with no partner should be thrown out.

* Use storage baskets in the entrance areas and keep all of your gloves, hats and scarves together, so you won't put on your boots, realize you have no gloves or a hat to hand, and then traipse through your house in your muddy boots looking for them.

* Keep matching sets together – each family member can have their own basket or canvas bag to keep their warm accessories organized.

★

Say "no" to shoes

Make a rule that shoes come off as soon as anyone comes inside. Think about it: if those dirty soles stay in the entrance hall, you greatly reduce the amount of mud, salt and water that gets tracked through your house.

* Place a large storage tub at the entrance so shoes can be popped in easily. If you get home first, ramp up the "welcome home" factor by having a fresh pair of warm socks or slipper socks waiting for family members when they return from school or work. That way, all the feet that tread through your house are not only clean but also cozy.

* As an alternative to the large tub, leave a small shoe rack in the entrance. With the rack as a prompt, guests will be more inclined to remove their shoes and, in turn, keep your carpets clean.

★

Get party-ready

Winter is a time for plenty of indoor parties and social gatherings, so you will want the wine glasses to look top-notch – they need a little more attention than normal glasses to avoid water spots and streaks.

* Once you have washed the glasses in warm water with a dash of white wine vinegar, polish them with a microfibre cloth. For the best results, this should be done while the glasses are still hot and steamy, ideally directly from the washing-up bowl.

* Make sure to give your cutlery a good polish and remove those water marks – this can be achieved by rubbing with a banana or potato peel, then give them a buff with a microfibre cloth.

★

Pay attention to your pets

You're not the only one treading dirt into the house! Our pets don't have the luxury of footwear and are directly exposed to the elements – their little paws walk directly through the mud and puddles.

* If your household has a pet, it is going to need a bit more cleaning attention than a house without one. Keep an old towel at your entrance and after a lovely winter walk or a good play in the garden, use the towel to give your pet a once over, drying their coat and all four paws individually.

* By brushing their coat on a regular basis, you help remove any excess pet hair that would otherwise shed around the house.

★

Protect your footwear

Our shoes go through a lot in the winter, protecting our feet from the snow, rain, mud and more. If you want to prolong the life of your shoes, there are a few different ways that you can make them more resistant to the harsh winter weather.

* How you protect your shoes depends on the type of material. Leather shoes should be polished as often as possible, whereas suede should be coated with a shop-bought protective spray and brushed regularly.

* Keep a basket of shoe-care items in your household supplies cupboard.

* Some trainers can be cleaned in the washing machine. Use a mesh laundry bag to protect them and wash at a low temperature. Dry them underneath a radiator, not on the top.

★

Clean the inside of your oven

Admittedly, this is not the most pleasant cleaning task, but it has to be one of the most satisfying. You don't realize how filthy your oven has become until you clean it – and then you realize that the oven door actually has a window.

* Sprinkle the oven door with bicarbonate of soda and then spray with white wine vinegar. Leave for at least 30 minutes and then rub away all those burned-on bits with a damp cloth. No harsh chemicals or intense elbow grease are needed, and the grimy residue fizzes away.

★

Smoke detectors

Wipe down any smoke detectors that may be in your home and then replace the batteries and test to make sure that they work. Also check all carbon monoxide detectors to make sure they are functioning.

★

Winter bedding

Take out your winter bedding, duvets and any throw blankets. Wash them or take to the dry cleaners to freshen up and then store the summer ones away. Use vacuum bags for easy storage.

★

Dust

Homes get extra dusty in the winter because the air is so warm and dry.

* Dust your home's surfaces from top to bottom to help keep the dust to a manageable level. Don't forget ceilings – an easy way to dust them is to flip a flat mop upside down and work along the ceiling in strips.

★

Clean the windows

If you have a fireplace or burn candles, your windows are likely to get a little thin layer of soot over the winter months, which can block out the much-needed winter sunshine.

* Give all your windows a good wipe down weekly using a solution of water and vinegar and buff with a microfibre cloth.

★

Clean your radiators

You need to keep your home warm during this time. One of the most common reasons for a freezing room is not bad insulation, but dirty radiators.

* Use a long-armed radiator cleaning brush to clean the inside and to stop the dust from settling. Wipe over the front panel on a weekly basis. You will probably notice a difference straight away after cleaning.

★

Switch to steam cleaning

Steam cleaning is perfect for the winter months (though commendable all year round). It is a completely natural, chemical-free and eco-friendly way of cleaning, and eliminates germs and viruses in your home.

★

Stock up your kitchen cupboards

Winter is the time to stock up on different foods to avoid going out in the cold weather throughout the week.

* Organize your kitchen cupboards ahead of time to determine the canned and dried foods that you already have and any ingredients that you need to purchase for recipes you plan to make.

* Use stacked organizers for cans, which make items easy to find, instead of allowing them to get lost on the back of each shelf. Check expiry dates and donate any items you know you aren't going to use to the local food bank.

Keeping your cupboards in order and knowing what you have stops you from spending money on duplicate items and will lower your food-shopping bill.

★

Store documents electronically

Dark and rainy days are the perfect opportunity to de-clutter all of the documents and paperwork that you've accumulated throughout the year.

* Free up extra space in your filing cabinet to prevent records from getting lost – this will save you time when you need to find a specific document in minutes, and can also prevent you from losing important receipts or transactions.

★

Cleaning welly boots

Dealing with dirty wellies in winter can be a real pain. Wellies easily pick up dirt from all that tramping around in the mud and snow.

In order to prevent things like holes and tears, it's important to ensure that our wellies are kept clean and are looked after well. Of course, wear over the years is to be expected, but taking good care of your boots can lead to them lasting longer than usual. Cleaning boots can be messy, so try and do this outside on a dry day.

* Grab yourself a clean rag or a hard brush and wipe off any debris your boots have picked up, such as dirt, grass and mud. Start at the top of your boots and work downward, cleaning the sole last.

* Prepare yourself a bucket of warm soapy water, soak a clean rag or cloth in it, and work in a circular motion to clean the boots. For the soles, use an old toothbrush to get the dirt out of the grooves.

* If you have any scuff marks, gently rub with a standard eraser. If this fails, try toothpaste applied with your finger.

★

Wet wellies

If your wellies get absolutely soaked on a rainy walk or dunked in a river, you need to dry them out as soon as you get home.

* Always air-dry your wellies. Don't put them on top of radiator or in the tumble dryer. Find a suitable place to leave them and sit them on an old towel or a piece of newspaper. Putting them in direct sunlight is also not a good idea because this can damage the rubber.

* The most effective way to dry sodden wellies is to scrunch up some old newspaper and pop it inside each boot, removing after a few hours. The newspaper will soak up the damp. Repeat until fully dry.

★

Candle safety tips

Candles are the perfect accessory for your home over the colder dark nights and can help bring coziness to any room. An assortment of candles of varying heights, bundled together (when unlit), can make a lovely autumnal feature for your lounge or dining area.

To enjoy your candles safely, you do need to be careful and keep safe. Here are some tips to help.

* When you are using candles, make sure they are secured in a proper holder and away from materials that may catch fire, like curtains, Christmas trees, decorations and toys.

* Never leave young children and pets alone with lit candles. Try to keep candles up high rather than on low surfaces like coffee tables.

* Always put candles out when you leave the room, and make sure they're extinguished completely before you go to sleep.

* Make sure you trim the wick each time before burning. Long or crooked wicks can cause uneven burning, dripping or flaring.

* Never move candles once they are lit, as they can be extremely hot, and you risk dropping them or tripping over something.

* Follow the manufacturer's recommendations on each candle's burn time – they are there for a reason.

* Do not burn several candles close together because this might cause flaring (mainly with tea lights).

* Always make sure tea lights are placed in a proper holder. The foil container that tea lights come in can get so hot that they can melt through plastic, such as a bath, and have the potential to start a house fire.

* Ensure you have a working fire alarm in your home when using candles.

* Use a snuffer or a spoon to extinguish candles. It's safer than blowing them out and risking flying embers.

* Make sure that everyone in your home knows what to do in the event of a fire, and that they know where to find the nearest fire extinguisher and exit.

* With candles in jars or glass containers, never pick up the hot glass that has housed a burning candle until it has cooled sufficiently.

★

Looking after your family car

In addition to looking after your home through the winter, you need to give your car some attention, too. No one wants to break down on a cold, dark, wintry night. Keep your family safe this winter by doing a few checks to make sure it is running well. Most garages offer a winter check these days. If you would prefer to do this yourself, follow these simple steps.

★

Change your oil

This is something you should be doing whenever it's needed, but in the winter months it's especially important.

* You may need to change the type of oil you use altogether. Check your car manual to find out what you should be using in freezing temperatures.

* You want to make sure the battery is functioning properly. Start by making sure you have enough charge left in your battery. The simplest way to check is by turning on your headlights before you start your engine. Then turn your engine on – if the lights get brighter, your battery may be dying.

★

Change your washer fluid and windshield wipers

* Buy a good washer fluid with an antifreeze solution for the winter months.

* Check to see if you need to replace your windshield wipers. These usually need to be replaced every six months to a year.

★

Check your heater

* Make sure your heater is functioning properly in order to drive safely in the winter. One tip that may save you money on a defroster system repair is to check for air leaks around doors and windows. Leaks can allow in extra moisture that make it seem like you have a broken defroster.

* Keep a can of de-icer by the back door so it's at hand when you leave for work on the cold dark mornings. Keep a few backup cans in your household cupboard.

★

Inspect your tyres
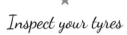

Look at the tread on your tyres for wear and tear as well.

★

Keep a car emergency kit

If you don't already have an emergency kit in your car, now is the time to get one! If you do have one, you may want to add a few things for the winter just in case you break down.

* Keep a box in the boot with a few blankets, a torch, an old coat, gloves and some water.

Keeping your home germ free

With winter comes the cold and flu season. People will be coughing in supermarkets, on trains and in the office, and the germs will be flying around and unexpectedly hitting us.

During the colder months it is very important to make sure we try to keep our homes germ free. There are a few basic steps we can all do to help stop the spread of germs.

★

Hand washing

It still baffles me that people don't wash their hands as they come out of the toilet! Washing your hands is crucial to stop the spread of germs.

* The best way to wash your hands is with warm soapy water. While washing, pay particular attention to the area between your fingers and slowly count to 20, the recommended threshold for killing most bacteria.

* Wash them as soon as you come in the house – when you are out and about, you touch a variety of germ hotspots, including door handles, shopping trolleys, shopping baskets, coffee tables and keyboards.

* Keep a small bottle of hand sanitizer in your handbag or pocket and use this when you don't have access to a sink and soap. Hand sanitizer won't kill all the germs, but it is certainly better than nothing.

★

Wipe down sides and door handles in your home

Use an antibacterial spray and cloth to wipe down items people touch frequently, such as phones, door handles, drawers, work surfaces, tables, remote controls, the fridge door, toilet handles and seat, light switches, computer keyboards and so on. If you can, try to do this daily.

★

Soft furnishings

Take a look at all the soft surfaces in and around your home. You come into contact with blankets, pillows, pillowcases, bed sheets and couch cushions. All of these need washing frequently, as do doormats.

★

Put the toilet seat down when flushing and not in use

Toilets are some of the most germ-ridden places in your home. You must deep-clean your toilets at least once a week, and take a couple of other steps.

* Try to put down the lid of your toilet seat prior to flushing to prevent bacteria-laden water from landing on other surfaces in your bathroom, where it can survive for a couple of hours. The germs from an open toilet can even hit your ceiling. For this reason, do not store your toothbrush near your toilet.

* Use a good toilet brush that keeps germs safely locked away and regularly soak the brush in bleach. Rather than using bleach daily, rotate it with denture tablets, which sterilize the toilet pan and keep limescale at bay.

★

Disinfect your cleaning cloths and sponges

Wash these after every use. There are a few simple ways to keep these clean.

* Put them in the dishwasher on the top shelf, pop them in the microwave for a few minutes, soak them in boiling water and a disinfecting product while you are out or put them in the washing machine on a hot wash. The higher the temperature, the better, as heat kills bacteria.

★

Shoes off

Do not let anyone wear shoes in your house. Leave a basket near the front door and encourage guests to remove their shoes. You don't want any mud and dirt coming into your home and spreading germs. If anyone is resistant to taking their shoes off (perhaps due to health and safety regulations or because they are a tradesperson), offer them some shoe covers.

★

Carpet cleaning

Try to get into the habit of cleaning carpets once a quarter and refreshing on a regular basis. For my homemade carpet refresher recipe, see page 188.

* Hire a machine, employ a company or invest in your own carpet cleaner. My advice is to invest in a machine because you will save yourself money in the long run, especially if you share the cost with a family member or neighbour.

* The benefits of carpet cleaning include: longer-lasting carpets; eliminating stains that you have missed over the months; reducing visible tracks from high-traffic areas; and improving the overall appearance of your carpeted rooms.

★

Bedding and towels

* Regularly change bedding and towels and avoid sharing them.

* When finished with your towel, hang it and keep the bathroom window open so your towel airs out and dries.

★

Wash children's toys

One of the most common places where germs are found in the home is on children's toys that are used each day. Children can easily get sick and catch the flu during the winter season when they play with items that are not cleaned on a frequent basis. To quickly clean the toys without spending a lot of time or money, stick plastic toys in the dishwasher or in a mesh bag in the washing machine. Wash soft toys in the washing machine too. If they are delicate, pop them in a bag and leave in the freezer a few hours.

★

Use a humidifier

Winter air is quite dry, and humidifiers put moisture back in the air. They improve sleep, keep your skin hydrated and looking fresh, help you breathe better and cough less and they improve sinuses. If you do end up getting the flu or an infection, the humidifier can help you heal more quickly.

While humidifiers are fantastic for you for a number of reasons, they do need to be cleaned regularly. Otherwise, they can become a source of bacteria and mould, which you don't want airborne in your home.

Drying laundry in the winter

Now the winter is upon us, you will use your tumble dryer a lot more often since drying on the line during the winter months isn't always possible (unless you get one of those rare windy days with a sunny blue sky). Getting your laundry done when you no longer have the facility of the washing line can be a real pain.

We are left with not many options and one is to air-dry our clothes indoors, but numerous recent scientific studies have shown that this can be unhealthy and cause mould. Make winter laundry more bearable with my helpful solutions.

★

Tennis tricks

Running a tumble dryer can be expensive. I highly recommend putting a few clean tennis balls or dryer balls into the drum to speed up drying time and prevent clothes from getting tangled. As an added bonus, the dryer balls also give off a fresh scent.

★

Create a drying space

If you are lucky enough to have the space, choose a spare bedroom or unused room in which to keep your clothes horse.

* Keep the room well ventilated. Open the windows and shut the door so the fresh air can circulate. Rotate the laundry a few times a day, and pay special attention to areas such as cuffs and underarms, which take longer to dry.

* Remember: when using a drying rack or clothes horse that has individual bars, hang items over two bars instead of one so more air can circulate.

* The electric clothes horses that you can now buy allow your clothes to dry more quickly and, surprisingly, don't use up much electricity.

Run an extra spin after your washing cycle has finished

When your laundry cycle has finished, run an extra spin at the maximum spin speed. You'll be surprised at how much this can help with the drying time and how much more water is removed.

★

Hang your garments

One of my favourite drying tricks is to put clothes on a hanger and then hang them on the curtain rail with the window slightly open.

* If you have a shower rail in the bathroom, you can hang your items here too. Clothes can dry more quickly than you'd expect like this, plus it makes them less creased and easier to iron.

* Good, strong hangers are essential to keep your garments in shape.

★

Dehumidifiers

A dehumidifier is another great option to help dry clothes. Some of the newer models are so advanced that they have settings specially designed for drying clothes. Their main purpose is to remove excess moisture from the air.

★

Portable electric clothes dryers

These energy-efficient, simple and easy-to-assemble dryers are impressive alternatives to the tumble dryer. They release gentle warm waves of air and can be left on overnight.

★

Do not overload radiators

Don't hang clothes on the actual radiators; this makes your boiler work harder and increases your heating bills. Instead, opt for radiator airers – you will also find that the clothes crease less.

★

Seize the sunny winter day

Yes, you can still dry your clothes outside in the winter! I love my washing line and still believe the best way of drying clothes is outside. I hang some of my washing out to dry outside if it's a cold, sunny winter's day.

* Light items such as shirts and bedding will dry if they are outside for the majority of the day, but when you bring the washing in, it will feel cold.

* By drying our clothes outside, we keep them fresh and well aired. This avoids moisture being trapped in the fibres, which encourages unpleasant musty smells.

* Putting clothes away clean and aired enhances the life of any garment over time, which means your favourites remain with you for longer.

Looking after your tumble dryer

Not everyone thinks to give their tumble dryer a clean, but trust me, it needs some regular attention when it's in use so often. Did you know that many household fires are caused by dirty clothes dryers? By keeping your dryer maintained, you can prevent this from happening.

After every use, make sure you remove any build-up from the lint filter. This keeps the dryer working efficiently and helps to keep winter energy bills down.

Before you remove the lint fluff, check your dryer has cooled to prevent any burned fingers.

Every so often, take the filter and soak it in some warm, soapy water to give it an extra clean and check for any signs of damage that can sometimes occur. If damage has occurred, these are cheap and easy enough to replace.

While the lint tray is out, use your vacuum nozzle to remove any overflowing dust and fluff. If you can access the back of your machine, giving this a little attention as well.

Clean the drum and the dryer seals using a damp cloth and your favourite cleaning product. When cleaning the inside of your tumble dryer, it's important to think about safety; I advise that you unplug the dryer prior to cleaning.

Keep the outside of your tumble dryer clean by giving it a wipe with a damp microfibre cloth.

Remember that dryers can become damaged if they are overfilled, and can overheat.

Christmas and festive holidays

The winter holidays are a magical time when we celebrate being with loved ones and the start of a new year. But for some people, the additional tasks and pressure added to an already busy routine can be one big headache. Don't ever let the festive season stress you out. It is supposed to be a happy time enjoyed with family and friends. Take your time with it and start to prepare early.

I sometimes pick up the odd present in the January sales and keep them hidden away in a suitcase, with a note in my diary so that I don't forget what I have already bought. I did once forget and ended up gifting my daughters Christmas-tree-shaped bath bombs for their birthday in June! The look they gave me was a real picture. I suppose realistically I could have saved them for the following Christmas.

Start to plan your holiday celebrations as early as October, and set yourself a weekly task to do so that you stay organized and on top of things.

★

Christmas to-do list

Create a family to-do list and put it somewhere everyone can see (on the fridge is normally a great place). It may include the following tasks:

* Set your festive budget. Ask people what they actually want as a gift from you, or at least a few ideas. Buying what people want and need helps with your budgeting as well.

* Book panto tickets and a slot to see Father Christmas.

* Mark social activities down so you don't double-book with people and remember to hire babysitters if you have small children.

* Don't forget school activities, such as the nativity play or carol concert.

* Buy a few presents every week and keep a chart of what you are buying and how much you have spent. This is easier than cramming the gift shopping into one day; I can guarantee you will forget items and need to hit those shops again.

* Buy a few extra gifts for those unexpected guests or neighbours that end up gifting you something.

* Buy plenty of wrapping paper, gift tags and Sellotape.

* Check your supply of batteries. The last thing you want is to run out over the holiday itself, when no shops are open.

* Order the turkey and make sure it will fit in your oven if you are hosting Christmas Day, or decide on a vegetarian alternative and research recipes.

* If you have young children, or even sneaky teenagers, work out some suitable hiding places for the presents you buy.

* Set a date to send out your holiday cards. Don't forget to allow extra time for any overseas cards.

* Plan festive meals. Book in food delivery slots for before Christmas and after, so that you have enough supplies in for New Year celebrations.

* For all your festive social gatherings, you are going to want something nice to wear. Look through your wardrobe and set aside those outfits or go and treat yourself to something new. The sparklier, the better – after all, it's not every day you can get away with wearing glitter and sequins! Make sure the children have something that fits too.

* Set aside time to put the decorations up. This can be a lengthy process and may need the whole household to pitch in. Delegate jobs so it's easier and quicker, and pop on those Christmas carols to get in the festive mood.

* Try and stick to one decorative theme throughout your home, if you can.

* Plan pet care for your beloved animal if you're going away.

* Don't forget that big Christmas clean. If you've planned a few social gatherings at yours and have a guest or two staying over, the last thing you want is an untidy, disorganized house. There is always the annoying relative that finds something to criticize you for, so don't give them the satisfaction.

* Prepare a guest room or space and make sure they have all simple essentials to make their stay as comfortable as possible. Write the WiFi code down for them, leave them a set of clean, fluffy towels and create a space in a wardrobe or provide a clothes rail for their garments. Add a bunch of flowers to give a comfortable, homely feel.

* Plan to have your carpets cleaned before Christmas. If you are using a carpet-cleaning service, get this booked in as early as October. If you have your own, just set aside a few hours to get those carpets looking as good as new.

* Focus on the windows and window frames and tidy up cupboards and drawers.

* Run around with a long-handled duster and dust the ceilings and corners to get rid of cobwebs, and then reach down low and dust those skirting boards.

* When cleaning, always start at the top and work your way down; dust falls like snow.

* Keep extra drinks somewhere cool like the garage or shed, and create a cupboard in the kitchen for extra snacks such as crisps, cheese balls and Twiglets.

* Change any candles and reed diffusers in your home to Christmas- or winter-scented ones, and if you have any seasonal scatter cushions and throws, now is the time to get these back out, along with any festive bedding that you may have.

* Buy some compostable plates and cups – these are often useful over the festive period, as they save on the washing up. Try looking for bamboo.

Fridge-cleaning Step-by-Step

Fridges look after our food, but do we look after our fridges? Your fridge and freezer need a little TLC to be ready for all the extra food and drink you'll be getting in over the festive holidays. On the lead-up to Christmas, write a list of what you actually have in your freezer and start eating it, so you make space for the holiday influx.

Use my Fridge-cleaning Step-by-step as a guide:

☐ Step 1 – Empty the fridge

☐ Step 2 – Check use-by dates

☐ Step 3 – Throw out any mouldy or off foods

☐ Step 4 – Soak the shelves and compartments in warm soapy water with a drop of white wine vinegar, which acts as a deodorizer

☐ Step 5 – Clean all the fridge walls with a soapy water solution

☐ Step 6 – Clean in between the rubber seal: cover a blunt knife with a microfibre cloth and dip into the warm soapy water, then work up and down

☐ Step 7 – Place a dish of bicarbonate of soda towards the back after cleaning, to soak up odours

☐ Step 8 – Clean the outside of the fridge and the top

☐ Step 8 – Buff the outside dry using a microfibre cloth

☐ Step 9 – Put the food back in

☐ Step 10 – Stand back and admire

Christmas To-do list

Cleaning tasks

Food, drink & nibbles

Christmas Eve

Christmas Day

Boxing Day

New Year's Eve

Other

Festive outfits

Christmas cards

Decorations

Gifts

NOTES

New Year's declutter

With an entire new year ahead of you, your home should look good, feel good to live in, and attract all good things to you, so it's time for a declutter.

After your New Year's thorough declutter, your home should be feeling more spacious and, more importantly, you should be feeling more capable of maintaining a clutter-free space. With a cluttered house, you don't function as well as you could, and you want to go into the new year fully motivated and ready to take on the world. Leave the past in the past and move forward.

Try to get the other members of your household involved. They might not be interested, but don't try to force them. Hopefully, they will see the positive changes happening around the house and change their tune and pitch in!

* The week between Christmas and New Year's Eve is often a little quiet, so this is actually a really good time to start to go through bits and pieces. There is plenty to clear out, from Christmas leftovers to worn-out clothing.

* You don't need to save boxes from every gift you got this year. Go through them, save the ones you really do need, salvage any important parts or papers and then recycle the rest so they don't take up unnecessary space.

* If you're ready to replace your old artificial tree or you don't like your decorations anymore, help make someone else's Christmas brighter and happier by donating them instead of throwing them away. Check with local charities to see what they accept, and recycle or throw away what is left over.

* If you have kids, this is now a perfect time to donate some of their old unused toys, since there may be some new ones on the scene. Your kids won't miss them, and you'll make a lot of other kids really happy (or make your kids some extra pocket money if you manage to sell any).

* It's not just your home you want to declutter. Remove any negativity from your life: it may be time for a career change or time to evaluate the people around you.

★

Bedrooms and wardrobes

* Open up the wardrobe, take everything out and sort your clothes and shoes into three piles – keep, donate, and throw away. Only put back what you need and are going to wear. To help with space, use hangers that are all the same, rather than a mixture. Store shoes neatly at the bottom or in shoe-storage bags that fit under the bed.

* Go through drawers holding underwear, PJs and socks and do the same. If a sock is missing its mate or is damaged, throw it away or put it in a pile to take to your local clothing or fabric recycling.

* If you use the underneath of your bed for storage, get this all out and evaluate in the same manner.

* Declutter perfumes and any accessories you have, too. Make sure to check if your perfumes have expiry dates, and if these have passed.

* Sometimes our windowsills can really build up with clutter, from picture frames to candles. Just give these a once-over and remove any items you're no longer attached to.

★

Kitchen

* Chuck away worn-out tea towels and dishcloths, or make into rags and use for outside cleaning and car cleaning.

* Sort through your kitchen's small appliances, such as hand blenders and bread makers. If you haven't used these in the last year, it is time to sell or give them away.

* Check your food cupboards. Throw away any expired foods and spices, and donate what you know you won't eat to the food bank.

* Take stock of cookware. Check for wobbly handles on pots and pans and, if the problem is unfixable, it's time to say goodbye. Check plate sets and

mugs and try to keep only what you as a family need, with a few spares for guests.

* Tupperware time. If lids are missing or stained with food, it is time to toss them. Keep only what you need and store what you keep neatly. You do not need to keep every single plastic takeaway box. Alternatively, think of ways to reuse these around the home. If you also have a collection of plastic cups collected from fast-food restaurants, decide if these are truly needed and if they are not, toss them too.

* Most kitchens have a bits-and-bobs drawer full of little pieces with no real home. Be ruthless in going through this – most of it is probably not needed.

* Lastly, don't forget cleaning products. You may have many more now than you need. Take stock and re-evaluate, and as you move into the new year, try and make up your own products to reduce chemical usage and plastic.

★

Defrosting the freezer

Most freezers these days don't require the huge job of defrosting. I remember helping my mum do this often when I was young. Modern freezers are great, but they can use more energy than the manual-defrost models, and their auto-defrost cycle sucks all the moisture out of frozen food, which can affect food quality. If your freezer does require defrosting, use the following tips to make it quick, easy and efficient.

* Make sure you turn off the power to the freezer before defrosting.

* Empty out your freezer and have a sort through the food, putting what you're keeping into iceboxes.

* Leave the freezer door open to melt the ice. This can take a while, so make sure you leave a few old towels on the floor to soak up the water. If you haven't got time to wait for the ice to melt naturally, place in a few pans filled up with boiling water inside to help speed up the process.

* Once all the ice has gone, give the freezer case a good clean. I find warm

water and washing-up liquid works well. If you have nasty food smells, mix bicarbonate of soda and water into a paste. Rub this all over and then leave for approximately 30 minutes to allow the bicarbonate to soak up the odours. Clean all the shelves and any drawers the same way and ensure they are fully dry before you put your freezer back together.

* Once it's clean, you can switch it back on. Leave it for a while to get chilly again and then put the food back in neatly.

* If you don't have the hassle of having to defrost your freezer, give it a good clean with warm soapy water and then dry it well before putting the food back in.

★

Freezer organization

Your freezer is a cold and desolate place that's likely home to forgotten, icy food in unlabelled containers, which is wasteful.

* Make some labels, featuring the date the food went into the freezer as well as the number of servings, to identify your frozen leftovers. When you put in new food, bring the older food to the front so it doesn't get forgotten about. Categorize your shelves: have one for fish, one for meat and one for leftover portions so you know exactly what you have and can clearly see what meals can be made for the week.

* Remove shelves if you don't need them. Many shelves and drawers are removable, which opens up the space for you to make it suit you.

* Keep frozen vegetables, bread and chips in the freezer drawers and use bag clips to save food from spilling out.

* Use square containers that are all the same size for freezing leftovers so they fit together well and take up less room.

* Ditch packaging where you can. Keep a regular inventory of what you have in your freezer by using a list, which you can stick on the inside of one of the kitchen cupboards.

Hallways, stairways and entrances

* Don't give in to the temptation to leave items on the stairs or on the floors in hallways. Retrieve items that have been left there and return them to their proper locations.

* If you're struggling for space and have clutter everywhere, invest in storage tubs for the year ahead. These are incredibly handy for shoes, gloves, scarves and dog leads and can be kept neatly by the door. You could also try a storage bench, which provides an entrance hall with storage for shoes and handbags, with the added extra of seating for when you are putting on that awkward pair of boots.

* Go through the pile of keys you have and make sure they are all relevant to you and your home. Keep keys neat by hanging them on hooks in the entrance area.

Living room

* Avoid magazine and newspaper racks that can get filled up easily – unless you commit to passing them on to a friend or recycling on a regular basis.

* Go through your shelves and sort through books, DVDs, CDs, candles and ornaments.

* Declutter side and coffee tables.

* If you have throws and cushions in your room and they are looking a little worn, reuse for a pet or for lying in the garden, and pick up a few new ones to help improve the tidiness of the room.

* Check under sofas and armchairs for any stray toys and sweet wrappers.

* Try to keep the living room as clutter free as you can so that it is easier to maintain tidiness.

★

Bathrooms

Bathrooms are notorious for collecting everything from expired medications to almost-empty bottles of soap and shampoo. As with any other room in the house, the first step to decluttering is getting rid of what's old.

* Empty the bathroom cabinet and sort through what you have. Empty bottles and any expired products need to go.

* Holding on to old make-up is something a lot of us are guilty of, but wearing products that are too old or expired can be bad for your skin – while you're in post-holiday cleaning mode, take the time to go through your beauty products.

* Empty drawers and the area underneath the sink, as well as any cabinets or shelves. If old toothbrushes have piled up, get rid of those, too. You'll

be surprised at how much space you suddenly have in your bathroom after a good New Year's declutter.

* Other solutions to keep your bathroom clutter free are to install a few hooks for towels. Carefully placed hooks make your bathroom more efficient.

* Use a closed-lid laundry basket so that dirty washing cannot be seen.

* The new year is also a good time to replace shower curtains.

* Keep a stash of cleaning products in your bathroom to save yourself running back and forth from the kitchen/laundry room.

★

Home office

* Sort through documents and scan in what you can. Once scanned, you can shred the original document, if appropriate.

* Organize the magnet board, getting rid of old receipts and letters that are no longer relevant. Attempt to make this a blank canvas ready for the year ahead.

* Add a family calendar to the wall to keep track of all events, commitments and overseas trips.

★

January Declutter Challenge

If all of this has been too much information to absorb, use my January Declutter Challenge and Deep-cleaning Checklist on the following pages and tackle an area a day.

Remember this quotation as you go into the new year:

"People don't eat well because their kitchen isn't functional, and they don't sleep well because their beds are piled with stuff."– Lynne Johnson, Institute for Challenging Disorganization

January declutter challenge

1	2	3	4
Fridge	Food cupboards	Kitchen drawers	Junk drawers

5	6	7	8
Tupperware	Pin board	Handbags/ school bags	School uniform

9	10	11	12
Towels and bedding	Toiletries	Windowsills	Make-up

13	14	15	16
Kids toys	Under-stairs cupboards	Coats and shoes	Paperwork

17	18	19	20
Under the beds	Mugs and glasses	Bookshelves	Medicine cabinet

21	22	23	24
Cleaning products	Porch/entrance area	Office desk	Kids arts and crafts

25	26	27	28
Magazines/ newspapers	Underwear drawers	Bedside cabinets	Freezer

29	30	31	
Utility room	Garage	Garden shed	

Deep-cleaning Checklist

Living room

- [ ] Dust furniture, shelves and picture frames
- [ ] Dust electronics, such as TV and game consoles
- [ ] Organize any clutter
- [ ] Organize books, magazines and DVDs
- [ ] Steam sofas and chairs
- [ ] Wash washable cushion covers
- [ ] Wash any throws
- [ ] Vacuum curtains and blinds using the correct attachments

Dining room/family room

- [ ] Dust furniture, skirting boards and picture frames
- [ ] Clean the table, including the legs and the underside
- [ ] Organize any clutter
- [ ] Wipe down chairs (if fabric, steam them and spot-clean stains)
- [ ] Polish any displayed silverware

Bathrooms

- [ ] Scrub shower walls and fixtures
- [ ] Scrub bath
- [ ] Take down shower curtain and wash/scrub shower screen
- [ ] Empty and wash bin
- [ ] Clean mirrors
- [ ] Scrub sink and taps
- [ ] Clean the toilet
- [ ] Clean the toilet brush
- [ ] Wash bath mats
- [ ] Clean out and organize cabinets
- [ ] Wipe down cabinets
- [ ] Clean bathroom fan and light switches

Bedrooms

- [ ] Dust furniture
- [ ] Vacuum headboard
- [ ] Vacuum curtains with the correct attachment
- [ ] Tidy up clothes
- [ ] Wash mattress protectors and pillow protectors
- [ ] Flip mattress
- [ ] Clean under bed
- [ ] Clean windows
- [ ] Dust skirting boards
- [ ] Dust ceiling
- [ ] Dust lampshades
- [ ] Clean mirror

Cupboards and wardrobes

- ☐ Sort clothing into piles: keep, donate and give away
- ☐ Take items that need dry cleaning to the cleaners
- ☐ Organize items
- ☐ Dust any shelving
- ☐ Make sure hangers are all the same direction
- ☐ Vacuum where shoes have been

Home office

- ☐ File documents and papers
- ☐ Back up and delete old computer files
- ☐ Organize cabinets and drawers
- ☐ Refill office supplies
- ☐ Dust furniture and computer station
- ☐ Clean window and seal

Hallway

- ☐ Clean doormat
- ☐ Dust furniture
- ☐ Organize shoes and coats

Kitchen

- ☐ Wipe all cabinet sides, fronts and tops
- ☐ Organize cabinets and drawers
- ☐ Check food dates
- ☐ Clean fridge and freezer
- ☐ Clean bin
- ☐ Scrub inside of microwave
- ☐ Wipe down tiles
- ☐ Clean oven and hob
- ☐ Wipe down appliances, including cords
- ☐ Scrub sink area
- ☐ Clean windows
- ☐ Clean cabinet baseboards
- ☐ Clean light fixtures and fittings

Utility room

- ☐ Clean washing machine
- ☐ Clean tumble dryer
- ☐ Wipe down exterior of washer and dryer
- ☐ Organize cleaning supplies
- ☐ Clean doors
- ☐ Clean light switches

Garage

- ☐ Sweep floor
- ☐ Clean any oil spills
- ☐ Organize tools
- ☐ Organize toys and sports equipment
- ☐ Clean any surfaces

Winter To-do List

Priority tasks

....
....
....
....
....
....
....
....
....
....
....
....
....

Texts and emails to send

Shopping list (food and household essentials)

....
....
....
....
....
....
....
....
....
....
....
....
....

Phone calls to make

Cleaning tasks

What's for tea?

NOTES

Lynsey's tips and tricks

Reducing plastic in your home

With cleaning comes plastic bottles. Plastic is not good for our planet and we need to start reducing our plastic intake at home.

Plastic packaging isn't limited to cleaning products. Food, drinks, dry goods and beauty products also are usually housed in plastic. It's not easy to suddenly just cut plastic out of your life and home, but if you can start to make a few changes, you will be doing your bit for our wonderful planet.

★

A few things you can do

* Reuse any plastic bags you have, and keep a few in your handbag so you don't forget them when you go off to the shops – or use canvas bags.

* Most toilet roll comes in a plastic lining – reuse this to line your bathroom bin, or even better, toilet roll in paper packaging is available to buy online.

* When you are finished with your toothbrushes and mascara brushes, add them to your cleaning caddy as tools to tackle hard-to-reach areas.

* Takeaways tend to come in a plastic tub – if you have some left over, these can be fantastic for drawer organization, especially for smaller items such as paperclips, drawing pins and batteries.

* Though I have used plastic food/sandwich bags, I always rinse them out to reuse, and they end up lasting me ages. But you can easily find paper sandwich bags now, or even reusable cloth or beeswax ones.

* Buy some of your food from farmers markets. It is a great way to buy fresh, local produce without plastic. Take your own Tupperware and bags with you to pop your purchases in.

* Buy fresh bread to take away in paper bags or your own reusable bag.

* Switch plastic straws for metal ones and remember to take these out with you rather than take a plastic straw in a restaurant or a coffee shop. You can also say no to a straw if you don't need it!

* Buy products in cardboard or paper boxes rather than plastic bottles.

* Use matches or a metal lighter instead of plastic lighters for your candles.

* Make fresh smoothies and juices instead of buying juices in plastic bottles; it's healthier for you and for the environment.

* Use a razor with replacement blades, such as a safety razor.

* Use the old-fashioned wooden pegs rather than the plastic ones for hanging laundry, they actually last longer too.

* Say "no" to plastic cutlery. Opt for wooden cutlery or buy an extra set in stainless steel, which will last you for years of BBQs and garden parties.

Make your own cleaning products

Making your own cleaning products can be fun and is inexpensive. There are so many benefits as to why you should make a few of your own potions.

* Better air quality

* Better for the environment

* Safe to use around pets and children

* Cost-effective

* DIY cleaners do not trigger asthma or allergies

Here are a few simple options for you to easily make at home. All these homemade solutions are based on a 500ml bottle and can be kept up to three months.

You need:

* Glass spray bottles

* Self-adhesive labels

* Funnel

* Lemon juice

* White wine vinegar

* Bicarbonate of soda

* Essential oils

  * Tea Tree: disinfects and repels insects

  * Lavender: disinfects

  * Eucalyptus: disinfects and breaks down glue and tape residue

  * Peppermint: disinfects and repels insects

★ Carpet refresher

250 grams of bicarbonate of soda popped into a large plastic reusables freezer bag

20 drops of essential oil

Shake well and leave overnight in a dark place for the bicarb to absorb the scent of the essential oil.

The next day, before you vacuum, sprinkle your carpet refresher all over the area you want to refresh and leave for 15 minutes to allow the bicarb to soak up odours from your carpet. Then, vacuum up the mixture.

Don't forget to reuse the bag for next time. If you would prefer not to use a plastic bag, you can use an old jam jar.

★ Fabric refresher

2 tablespoons of bicarbonate of soda

20 drops of your favourite essential oil

I tend to make up two of these: a lavender mixture for the mattress, as this helps aid sleep, and a lemon mixture for refreshing rugs, sofas and curtains.

Fill the rest of the bottle with water. Shake, and it's ready to use.

★

Glass and window cleaner

20ml white wine vinegar

10ml lemon juice

Fill the rest of the bottle with water. Shake, and it's ready to use.

This amazing glass cleaner is fit for anything you would use a shop-bought glass cleaner for, such as mirrors, mirrored furniture, windows and even metal taps.

★

Multipurpose cleaner

20ml white wine vinegar

20 drops of essential oil (I like to use peppermint for this one)

Fill the rest of the bottle with water. Shake and it is ready to use.

I love this multipurpose cleaner for its versatility, which saves you so much space in your cleaning cupboard/caddy. You can use this product every day for shining results in your bathroom and kitchen, and throughout the house for cleaning up any messes.

Versatile household products

You'd be amazed by the products sitting in your bathroom and kitchen cupboards which can be used for cleaning. These are all affordable, easy to buy and easy-to-use products. Best of all, they're incredibly versatile, and can be used for many different tasks.

★

Rubbing alcohol

Rubbing alcohol is commonly found in our medicine cabinets and is used as a mild antiseptic. It's not perfect for every single cleaning task, but it is an environmentally friendly solution that is fantastic when used for a few tricky surfaces, so it deserves a space in your cleaning cupboard.

* Some cleaning products contain acid, which can cause marks on granite surfaces and strip away their seal. Rubbing alcohol is an inexpensive way to clean granite, and it leaves a wonderful shine. Simply mix 25ml rubbing alcohol into 200ml of water, shake and use. Then, buff the surface dry with a microfibre cloth to maintain that super shine.

* Keep your phone germ free with rubbing alcohol. Put some product on to a cloth and rub over the surface of the phone or tablet and then let it dry.

* Marker pen is one of the hardest stains to get rid of, especially from white school shirts. Spray rubbing alcohol directly on to the stain, let it sit for 15 minutes, rinse and then wash as normal. This also works on desk surfaces.

* Nail polish can transfer from your toes and hands on to your bathtub, and a spill on wooden floors can be disastrous. Pop some rubbing alcohol on to a cloth and simply rub them away – the stains and marks will vanish.

* Sticker goo will slide right off with rubbing alcohol.

* If you sit in front of a mirror when doing your hair, you are more than likely to get a little hairspray on your mirror. Rubbing alcohol gets this off easily.

* Spray rubbing alcohol in the sink to clean, disinfect and shine it up.

* Your keyboard and mouse are covered in germs – apply the product directly to a microfibre cloth and clean them up.

★

Shaving foam

Did you know that shaving foam isn't just for your skin? It is also a dynamic household cleaner with many applications.

Just be careful not to pick up shaving gel to clean, as this gives a different finish. Foam is the one to grab, and it doesn't need to be an expensive one. The supermarket own brands cost as little as 70p and work just as well, making this an inexpensive cleaner.

* It is absolutely brilliant for carpet stains – simply spray onto the stained area and then, with a damp cloth, really run the foam in. Let it dry. After a few hours, just vacuum it off.

* Shaving foam leaves behind a super shine on chrome and stainless steel surfaces. Apply the foam with a damp microfibre cloth, rinse off, and then buff the surface dry with another cloth.

* Using only a small amount directly applied to a cloth, clean dirty mirrors and windows, rinse and buff dry.

* To stop mirrors and shower screens from fogging when showering, wipe the mirror or screen with shaving cream and wipe it off with a dry cloth before showering.

* Use an old recycled toothbrush and a tiny amount of shaving foam to gently scrub jewellery, then buff dry.

* To keep glasses from fogging up, apply shaving cream to the lenses and wipe clean with a soft cloth.

* To clean, spray the oven with shaving cream, leave for 15 minutes to allow it to work and scrub with a scouring pad. Rinse with water.

* Spray shower doors with shaving cream and wipe with a clean, dry cloth.

* Work shaving cream into stains with a clean, damp rag. Let it dry and launder the item according to manufacturer's instructions.

* If you have a squeaky door that's driving you mad, grab your shaving cream. Rub it into the hinges to provide lubrication and the squeak will disappear.

* Shaving foam is gentle enough to keep suede looking like new. Just rub all over the suede and blot with a damp cloth. Allow the shoes to dry naturally.

* Finally, not so much a cleaning tip, but shaving foam is helpful for keeping younger kids entertained. Squirt all over a play table, add some drops of food colouring and let the kids' creativity flow.

★

WD-40

WD-40 is an unbelievable all-round cleaner. Most of us have a can somewhere in the garage rather than in the cleaning cupboard. If you do, now is the time to bring it in and try some of these wonderful uses.

The "WD" in WD-40 actually stands for water displacement, and the "40" represents the number of attempts it took the inventor to get it right. When using WD-40, be aware that it is flammable, mustn't be inhaled and must be locked away from children. Check the packaging for full safety instructions.

* Chewing gum can end up in the strangest places, one of which is your child's hair. Next time, don't panic and grab the scissors. Instead, simply spray the hair strands that the gum is attached to with WD-40 and comb out gently. Be extra careful not to spray too close to the face or skin, and make sure you're in a well-ventilated space.

* A direct squirt to an ink stain on clothes, including denim jeans, does

the trick. Let it sit 10 minutes and rinse well afterwards, or run the item through the washing machine.

* Banish scuff marks from patent shoes and kitchen baseboards.

* If your child has gone sticker happy and stuck them all over your glass windows, then they can easily be removed with WD-40.

* WD-40 is great for carpet stains, especially those tough pollen stains from lilies.

* It happens to us all, doesn't it? That dreaded moment when you step in dog poo. But the WD-40's "water displacement" function makes the mess just slide off. Spray your trainers and give it a few minutes before starting to clean off. An old toothbrush will also come in handy here to get inside the shoes' grooves.

* Oil spots can really ruin the appearance of your driveway, but WD-40 will soon banish them.

* Kids are known to draw on painted walls or mark them as they go up and down with their toys. WD-40 removes these without ruining your paintwork.

* There's nothing better at slowing you down than a stuck zip, especially on your jeans. Just spray to loosen.

* Remove those awkward tea stains on kitchen surfaces – simply apply and rub off with a sponge.

* Spray the product onto your garden spades and forks to make gardening easier.

* If your children have some stuck Lego bricks, you can part them using a little WD-40.

* Over the winter months, wax from candles can find itself on your carpets and walls. Use WD-40 to remove the wax with ease.

Tea bags

You can't beat a morning cup of tea to set you up for the day. But did you know that tea bags have some incredible applications outside of your cup?

Our love for tea in the United Kingdom is huge – we get through a staggering 165 million cups daily. Normally, once we have made our cuppa, we just chuck the tea bag straight into the bin, but shame on us! There are many unexpected ways to get more from your tea bags.

Because its tannic acid cleans and adds shine, tea has been used to help with household tasks throughout the centuries.

So, what else can be tea be used for?

* Air freshener: once you have made your cup of tea, dry out your tea bags and then add a few drops of your favourite essential oil to them to create an air freshener. To make this a bit prettier, pop it in a small drawstring favour bag and put around your home or in your car. Tea naturally absorbs odours, helping take away those pesky cooking smells or the sweaty smell from teenage bedrooms. Top up with essential oil every few days, or when you feel you need to.

* Stubborn food: used tea bags are an alternative to chemicals to help remove that baked-on food. Put your dishes in hot water and then chuck in a few used tea bags and leave for a few hours. The tea will break down grease and grime, saving your arm from all that scrubbing.

* Smelly shoes: pop a few unused tea bags inside your smelly shoes, trainers and football boots to soak up nasty odours. Leave overnight in a dry, warm place.

* Plant food: sprinkle used or unused tea from tea bags in your plant pots. The nutrients from the tea will be released into the soil when you water them, encouraging growth.

* Wooden furniture: boil some water, add in a few tea bags and allow the

water to cool. Once cooled, dip a microfibre cloth into the tea, wring out any excess liquid and use it to clean your wooden furniture. The solution lifts any stubborn sticky patches, too.

* Rust: have a rusty old bike in the garage? Why not try to bring it back to life using tea? Wipe a used wet tea bag over the rust and dry with a microfibre cloth. Depending on how bad the rust is, you may need to repeat this a few times. Also try this on cooking pots and pans.

* Smelly hands: chopping up garlic and cooking with spices can leave your hands smelling and even slightly stained. Rub damp, used tea bags over your hands and rinse to take any odours away.

* Sticky fingers: remove finger marks by simply wiping a damp tea bag over the area.

* Puffy eyes: place two used bags over your eyes to relieve tired, achey eyes. The tannins in the tea help to reduce puffiness.

★

Natural ways to get rid of mould

Mould and mildew love a humid environment, and grow rapidly if given the chance. Ventilating your home is key to preventing this. Always open vents or windows after showering to allow the bathroom to dry out.

To remove mould and mildew, you don't need to reach for harsh chemicals. There are quite a few natural remedies that kill mould and mildew and keep your home environment safe.

* Put some hydrogen peroxide into a spray bottle and spray directly on to the mouldy surface. Leave on for a good 15 minutes. Scrub clean, then rinse with a damp cloth and buff dry. Hydrogen peroxide also removes black mould marks from your clothes and fabric laundry baskets and is also helpful for removing those underarm sweat marks.

* White wine vinegar is a versatile household cleaner and my go-to product for any mould patches. Vinegar is such a powerful cleaner that it kills viruses and bacteria. You can dilute it with water and mix in a spray bottle to help ease the vinegary smell or add a few drops of essential oil. However, it works best applied directly to the mould, neat, and the smell disperses quickly.

* You can use shop-bought lemon juice – found down the baking aisle in a supermarket – or the juice of an actual lemon to combat mould. Squeeze or squirt directly on and allow to work for 30 minutes. Rinse and buff dry.

* Tea tree oil is more expensive than some other eco-friendly remedies. That being said, just a few drops mixed with 20ml of water lasts you a while. Spray the solution directly onto the mould, but do not rinse. This oil also has a strong but not unpleasant scent, which dissipates within a few days.

* Used together with water, bicarbonate of soda is effective at removing mould naturally. Dissolve the bicarbonate of soda into water and then spray directly on to the problem area. Let it sit, then scrub and wipe with a damp cloth. The best thing about bicarb is it has no strong scent.

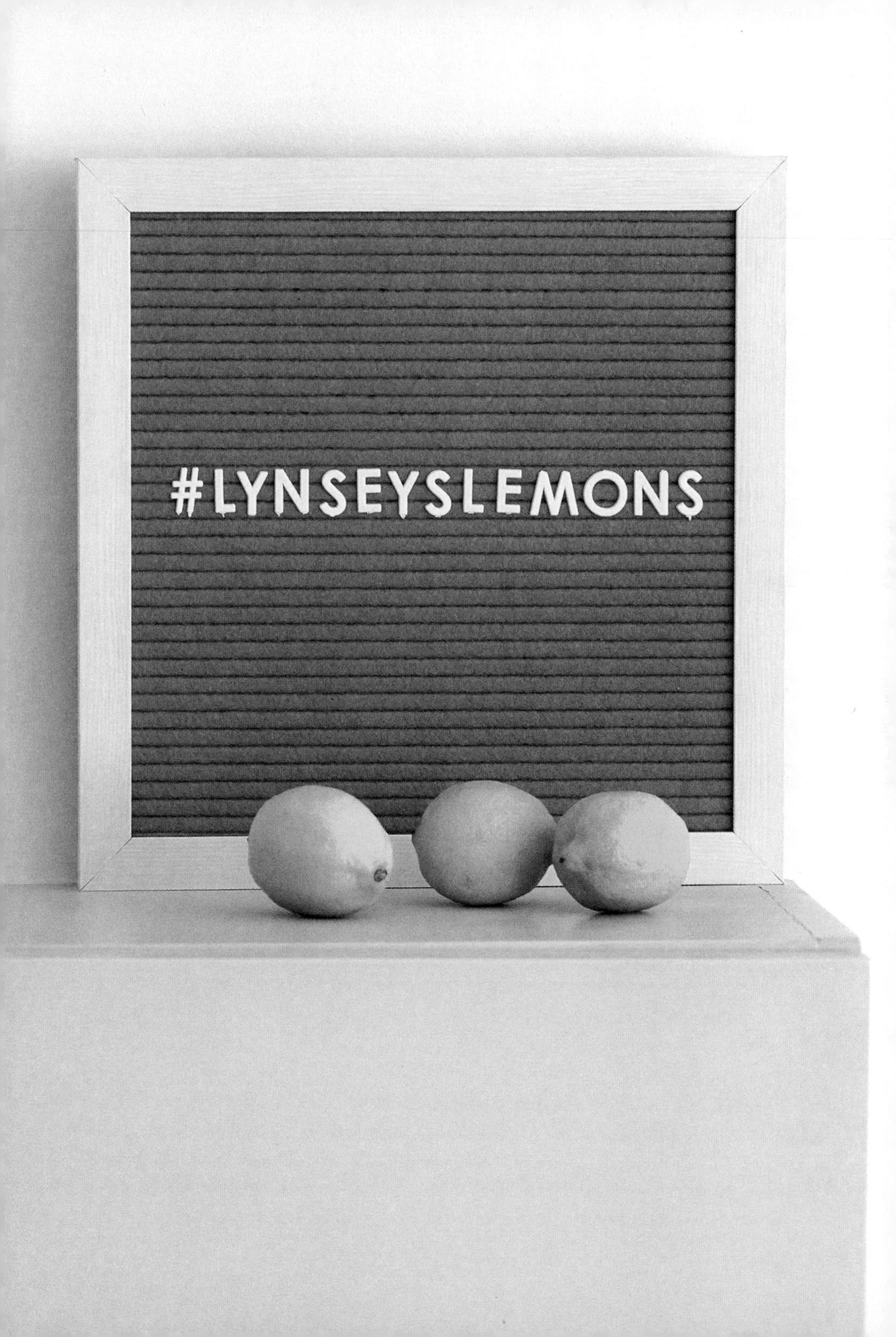
#LYNSEYSLEMONS

A – Z of quick and easy cleaning tips

I have pulled together some of my best cleaning tips and home hacks to help you keep a spotless home using the most eco-friendly methods, from the use of my favourite juicy lemons to cleaning with tin foil.

A

Alcohol, and vodka in particular, is a great all-round cleaner. It can remove marks, freshen and deodorize.

Aluminium foil has so many uses around the home. The best tip is to scrunch it up into a ball and scrub those pots and pans – a great way to recycle your sandwich wrapping.

B

Bath marks caused by nail polish on toes and bath toys can be removed using nail polish remover. Just remember to rinse with warm soapy water after you have used it.

BBQ grills aren't fun to clean, but a quick solution is to cut an onion in half and rub over the grills until it has disintegrated. The onion contains cleaning power that removes grease and grime.

Baby powder can stop squeaky floorboards. Drop some onto the floor and sweep into the cracks, then wipe away the excess.

C

Carpet odours quiver in the face of my simple eco-friendly carpet refresher. Fill a recycled jar with bicarbonate of soda, add 20 drops of your favourite essential oil, give it a good shake and leave overnight. Pierce holes into the top of the jar lid and liberally sprinkle over carpet. Leave 30 minutes and then vacuum off.

Creased clothes can be sorted out with a quick spritz of starch spray and a strong pull.

Coffee rings on tables can be removed with olive oil.

D

Dishwashers need a little TLC every so often. Once a week, fill up the tablet compartment with lemon juice. I tend to use shop-bought lemon juice for this, which you can get from the baking aisle in supermarkets, and then run a rinse cycle.

E

Eggs can occasionally drop on the floor and break when you're in the middle of a Nigella moment. Picking up raw egg with a cloth or a napkin isn't easy, and it is messy. Instead, grab a slice of bread and soak up that messy egg.

F

Flowers add a pop of colour to your home. To keep them lasting longer, add a drop of lemonade, vodka or a copper coin into their water and just watch the difference. A little spritz of hair spray under the leaves will stop them from dropping off, too.

Finger marks come right off stainless steel with baby oil.

G

Garden furniture rust can be cleaned using tomato sauce. Dab some ketchup on to a wet cloth and rub – the rust will lift right off.

Grease comes easily out of clothes by adding lemon juice directly on to the stain, leaving for 15 minutes and then rinsing.

Grass stains can be removed with toothpaste.

H

Hand sanitizer can be handy in emergency stain situations. If someone spills a drink or drops chocolate on a t-shirt, simply use your hand sanitizer to remove the stain.

Hob racks get dirty with a build-up of spilled food, grease and grime from cooking. Put these in your dishwasher with white wine vinegar. Alternatively, fill the bath a little and then add in some white wine vinegar and leave to soak 30 minutes.

Hair conditioner adds shine to our hair, and it can do the same for cars. After washing, add a squirt of conditioner to the water bucket, rinse car and buff for a perfect finish.

I

Icing a cake can be messy, but pick up those smaller bits of icing dust with the larger bits of icing fondant.

J

Remove labels from jars with olive oil so that you can reuse them.

K

Kitchen cabinets that are high gloss can be buffed up for the perfect shine using window cleaner.

L

Lily flower pollen really gets you when it gets you, and has ruined many of my tops in the past. A quick fix is to spray with WD-40.

Lego pieces trap dust in kids' bedrooms, so recycle an old make-up brush to dust them clean.

M

Mould and mildew can easily be removed using vinegar. To prevent mould and mildew, keep rooms well ventilated.

Mirrors collect dust. Use an S-shape when polishing with a solution of water and vinegar so you grab all of that dust.

N

Nail polish remover is great at getting pen marks off leather bags.

Nail polish spillages can be removed using window cleaner.

O

Ovens can be cleaned using just bicarbonate of soda and white wine vinegar.

P

Pet hair can easily be removed with a wet rubber glove or a lint roller.

Q

Quick cleaning is great exercise.

R

Rubber seals on washing machines pick up mould quickly and leave a nasty smell. Use a toothbrush and a mixture of bicarbonate of soda and white wine vinegar and scrub away, then pop your machine on the rinse cycle.

Razor blades remove paint and sticky labels from glass.

S

Sun cream stains can easily be removed with white wine vinegar or eucalyptus oil.

Stains can be a real pain, but get to them quickly and most will come out. Don't immediately go for the hot water because it will set some stains – use cold water instead.

Sponges and cloths can be cleaned in the dishwasher or microwave.

Soap scum on shower screens can be prevented by adding a coating of shaving foam.

T

Toilet stains are often not removed by bleach; we need to remember that bleach is a whitening, and not always a cleaning product, and it's not the most eco-friendly substance. When you have brown marks or built-up limescale, pop a few denture tablets into the bowl, close the lid and leave a few hours or remove some of the water and add in a neat limescale remover.

U

Unclog a drain using bicarbonate of soda and white wine vinegar. Sprinkle the bicarbonate of soda onto the drain and then pour down the vinegar. Cover with a wet cloth as the two react with one another to clean the drain naturally. Wait five minutes and then run some hot water to clear it.

Underneath beds or cabinets is an important area to check when cleaning. When wiping down kitchen cabinets, be aware that sticky grease from cooking can build up on the underneath.

V

Vaseline can be used to shine up your shoes.

W

Wooden chopping boards can be brought back to life using half a lemon and some salt.

Walnuts removed from their shells and rubbed into scuffs and scratches can restore skirting boards and wooden tables.

X

Xmas is the most wonderful time of the year. Take some time off your household chores and enjoy spending time with your family.

Y

Yellow sweat patches on the underarms of shirts can be cleaned using hydrogen peroxide.

Z

Zap those household bugs away using your own insect repellent of water and lemon juice.

Conclusion

Breaking down your cleaning and home organization is the key to living an easy life. I really hope that reading this book will have helped you to give your homelife some structure and routine, allowing you to spend more time with your family and friends, and to enjoy your life!

I really hope that you will continue to use this book as a constant guide for tips and tricks. Rather than putting it away on a shelf, leave it somewhere easily accessible where you can grab it for some instant motivation, throughout the seasons.

As much as an annual spring clean is important, your homecare doesn't stop there, and if you are on top of your home the annual spring clean will be a breeze.

Using my strategies for cleaning and home management will change your life. My advice is never to get stressed when it comes to looking after your home – and always remember that if you write all your jobs down onto a piece of paper it will never seem as bad as it is when it's stored in your head. Keep on using the checklists and planners in this book for guidance and tick off your completed tasks as you go. When you have ticked all of your jobs, you will get an immense feeling of satisfaction. Design a cleaning routine that works for you – there is no right or wrong way, as long as it gets done.

Running a home doesn't have to be difficult if you follow my positive approach. Remember, cleaning doesn't have to be boring!

Don't forget to follow me across my social channels for more cleaning hacks and advice. I love hearing from my readers and am always happy to answer any cleaning-based questions.

A huge thank you for reading my book.

Lynsey

Index

CREDITS

All images © Welbeck Non-fiction Limited with the exception of page 104 Mallmo/Shutterstock, page 145 photograph courtesy of Cox & Cox & page 169 Faithie/Alamy Stock Photo.

Every effort has been made to acknowledge correctly and contact the source and/or copyright holder of each picture and Welbeck Publishing apologises for any unintentional errors or omissions, which will be corrected in future editions of this book.

Art direction: Amy Honour
Design: Katie Baxendale
Editorial: Isabel Wilkinson
Hair & makeup: Charlotte Gaskell
Illustration: Misha Gudibanda
Photography: Michael Wicks

The publisher wishes to thank the following brands for loaning or gifting their products for inclusion in this book:

Addis (www.addis.co.uk)
Greens of Highgate (www.greensofhighgate.com)
Matalan (www.matalan.co.uk)
Swan (www.swan-brand.co.uk)